Never Go Under Money

JERIAH

www.neverundermoney.com

Never Go Under Money
Copyright © 2020 Jeriah

ISBN: 978-1-7354235-0-0 (Paperback)
Printed in the United States of America.

Some references to historical events, real people, or real places are used fictitiously. Some names, characters, and places are products of the author's imagination.

Book cover design by Jeriah

Additional design by Dynastyy Animation and Design.

First printing edition 2020.
www.neverundermoney.com
jeriah@neverundermoney.com
tel:1-248-277-5590 cell:1-313-778-8141

Disclaimer

I am not a financial advisor; this is not financial advice. This book is presented solely for educational and entertainment purposes. The author and publisher are not offering it as legal, financial, or other professional service advice. While best efforts have been used in writing this book, the author and publisher make no representations or warranties of any kind and assume no liabilities of any kind with respect to the accuracy or completeness of the contents and specifically disclaim any implied warranties of merchantability or fitness of use for a particular purpose. Neither the author nor the publisher shall be held liable or responsible to any person or entity with respect to any loss or incidental or consequential damages caused, or alleged to have been caused, directly or indirectly, by the information or programs contained herein. No warranty may be created or extended by sales representatives or written sales materials. Every investment is different, and the advice and strategies contained herein may not be suitable for your situation. You should seek the services of a competent professional before investing in any security, property, asset or any product perceived to have or will have value.

WARNING: THIS BOOK WAS DESIGNED TO CHANGE YOUR LIFE IMMEDIATELY!!! TAKE THIS BOOK WITH YOU EVERYWHERE YOU GO AND USE IT AS A ROADMAP TO GET OUT OF DEBT, TO START A BUSINESS, TO BUILD YOUR FUTURE NO MATTER YOUR AGE. IF YOU DONT FOLLOW THE INSTRUCTIONS IN THIS BOOK PLEASE GIVE IT TO SOMEONE WHO WILL AND WATCH THEIR LIFE CHANGE......

CONTENTS

Testimonials

Wen I was in the 11th grade, my father sat me and my brother Jalen down and taught us about stock options. I was working and looking for ways to expand my streams of income, but I was not using my funds the right way. I sat down with my father and brought money I had saved up and we went over what I had to do to find a good stock, what to look for to buy, gauging charts, when to pull out etc. After listening, taking notes and applying what I learned in a little less than a week I had doubled my money. My father always told me, "Scared money don't make money," so now my money fearless.

-Jamal ll

The financial guidance I got from Jeriah was a simple 30 to 60 day financial fast where I stop spending on things I wanted for a month at first, then in two months; I managed to save an extra 150 to 250 in those months and now I keep thousands in my bank account.

-Eli

The information contained in this book is truly life changing. It is a commonsense approach for the beginner taking their first steps into the wide world of finance. If you have the courage and discipline to apply the strategies in these precious pages, you will find a chance to create generational wealth! This book is a must-read for anyone who wants to get off the sidelines and start making their money work for them. I have personally applied these techniques over the last year and have made 18.5% gains. I wish I got this information sooner!

- David Israel / President/ CEO / The King's Transport, INC

Jeriah played an integral part in me currently having my rental property asset. After the Financial Crisis in 2008, Detroit's economy was largely affected. In 2009, Jeriah advised me to buy a property, even if it needed updating, so it could benefit me later. Following his advice, I bought a property and completed remodeling projects while living there. Currently, the house is worth five times more than when it was purchased in 2010. I have also made it my rental property, so the residual income is a major bonus! I only wish I were able to buy more properties during that time.

Jeriah also educated me on trading stocks. In our school system, there was no curriculum about how to manage money, invest in the stock market, trading strategies, etc. Through much needed tutelage, I have started a Roth and

Traditional IRA through Fidelity, where I have scheduled deposits set up monthly. They are linked to an Index Fund that I predict will grow at least 12%

yearly setting me up for retirement. The information Jeriah has provided me with has been pivotal in my journey towards financial success!

- Jermaine

CHAPTER 1

NEVER GO UNDER MONEY

"The LORD maketh poor, and maketh rich: he bringeth low, and lifteth up".

1 Samuel 2:7

Imagine you at 80 years old sitting on your porch watching your grandkids run around on the front lawn. You recline back in your rocking chair, enjoying the scenery taken place at the moment. You start daydreaming, thinking back on your whole life and you ask yourself, "What could I have done differently, what are the things or people I would've stayed away from"? Now open your eyes and realize this is your chance; everything starts from now! Now is the time to do everything you would have done differently as if you were 80 years old, thinking back!

There is an old saying, "If I don't know where I'm coming from, where would I go"? In your lifetime, what is the total amount of *cash* you've *acquired* from childhood up until today? If you do not know, just do a rough estimation, add & combine the totals of every year for *everything*. I am talking about every cent that has ever touched your hands. Afterward, write down the number that represents the Most amount of money you've held in your possession at one time (whether it was in your pocket, suitcase, purse, bank account, etc. or combined). Then ask yourself from all these amounts of money and overall this time, how much is left my bank account as of today? I created this exercise to get you mad at yourself, seeing that most people have never taken the time to calculate just how much money they have blown away throughout their lifetime. Hopefully, this will give you a better appreciation for your money and in turn, a greater appreciation for the information you are about to receive in this book.

Those two numbers that must be identified are the numbers that you need to see visually with your eyes written down on paper so that you can consciously internalize the most important financial achievements in your lifetime thus far. The one being the *Most* money you've ever had at one time (money that was yours and no one else's). The other number will be the *Grand Total* of ALL the monies you've ever touch in your life combined!

This will be the foundation we build on in the creation of your master plan to make sure you never go under money again.

Allowances from parent's _____

Financial gifts _____

Total wages from every job _____

Tax refunds (every year) _____

Business revenues _____

Real estate profit _____

Automobile sales _____

Jewelry sales / pawn _____

Bonuses _____

Lottery winnings _____

Casino winnings _____

Gambling winnings _____

Lawsuit payouts _____

Life Insurance payouts _____

Loans received _____

Cash found _____

GRAND TOTAL: _____

MOST MONEY AT ONE TIME: _____

From this day forward, every dollar you touch is your *employee* and just as bosses treat employees when they come to work ready and willing to do whatever task given to them. You will do the same to your employees, now what you won't do is say, "hey you, lay under my mattress and do nothing or better still, take an all-expense paid 6-month vacation to my local bank for absolutely no reason.

Money Don't Sleep, take naps, money don't take breaks, money don't need a vacation, money don't get sick, money never goes on maternity leave nor have to abide by any of the rules that us as human beings must abide by to thrive. We must get on a plane, bus, train, drive or take a boat to get out of our city or country to do work or do business but our employee "money" can get to any country or city in a matter of minutes, and in some cases seconds. This is done through wire transfers, banks and brokerages, Western Union, Money Gram, Cash App, PayPal, Cryptocurrency, Digital assets, blockchain technology and the list goes on and on; it all depends on what you are trying to accomplish.

While you are at work, your money should be at work, when you get off, your money should still be at work. When you go to sleep, your money should be up working. When you get fired from your job, your money should have made some friends and they all should be able to take care of you until you find another job. Now, none of this will be possible if you are a "spend artist" and lack the discipline when it comes to saving.

If you woke up today with $50, $500 or $5000 and you have a job or a business, this time next week you should have the same amount or more and realistically you should have more, but never less, my motto is "NEVER GO UNDER MONEY"!! Money should always be accumulating or at the least put up only until you find something to invest in.

I ask people all the time what do you invest your money in? The answers I hear the most are "nothing" or "I just put it in the bank." Two things are wrong with those statements:

1. You should always have your money invested in something!

2. Whether you know it or not, if your money is in a standard checking or savings account, you are already investing; but you do not get a return on your cash.

Another question I ask people is if they were to invest their money, how much do they expect to get in return and that is when the answers become outrageously unrealistic. One guy told me, he wants to double his money or get at least 60% - 70% percent extra, I'm like wow, this dude has absolutely no idea how investing works. Not saying these kinds of returns are not possible but just starting out, you must take baby steps and shoot for small gains at first. So, then I asked him if he had money in the bank and what was he investing in at the moment? He went on to explain how he didn't have any investments; he just had all his money in the bank, so I told him, you know you have all your money invested with a Retail bank right? Then I asked him how much interest is the bank giving him in return for using his money? He told me "nothing really," as I reminded him of how he just told me how he needed a 60% to 70% return on any investment...he laughed and replied "wow."

CHAPTER 2

BANKING 101

"He shall lend to thee, and thou shalt not lend to him: he shall be the head, and thou shalt be the tail."

Deuteronomy 28:44

What people do not understand is how banking works nor understand exactly what money is. Major banks only give out around 0.01% APY (Annual

Percentage Yield) on most interest checking accounts. The national average is about 0.04% and that is coming mostly from the high-interest rates of online banks and smaller regional banks whose account policies tend to be more generous to customers.

Now let us breakdown the cycle of a dollar and compare that info with how much the banks make off your money.

It is not an exact science, but one aspect of banking is similar to this: When you put $1,000 into your bank account, $900 of that the bank loans out to Johnny. Now Johnny takes that $900 and spends it on something such as a car, food, bill's or whatever. The company where Johnny spent that $900 takes it and puts it in the bank. Now the new bank can loan out $810 of that money. It is not new money but still part of the original $1,000 you put in. Of course, the cycle continues since that $810 is loaned out, spent, and then put into a bank by the recipient. The bank can then loan out $729 of that money. Now, if you paid attention, at each stage, money is being spent at some establishment and that business owner then puts into a bank. All the time, banks are earning interest as loans are repaid in amounts up to 1000 times what they pay you for the use of those funds. Also, that same $1,000 can be recycled repeatedly. Now, when you go to withdraw your $1000, ask your banker where's your percentage of those profits that were made off of your money, I'm sure they will kindly give you those pennies you agreed upon minus inflation and other fees.

Ask yourself how do banks make money? If you cannot answer that question then ask yourself why do you have your money deposited with them? Banks make money hand over fist due to government regulations, your ignorance, capitalism (everyone wanting to make a profit) and various other ways that you are not privy to. If a bank got a loan to open branches all across the country and after people deposited there checks 1 million of them over drafted their accounts, that would bring in roughly $36,000,000 dollars of revenue for that bank before it even opened its doors for business.

Banks took in around $11 billion dollars in 2019 in overdraft fees alone and what makes that even worse is 84% of those fees were paid by only 9% of account holders.

It has been said that banking can be summed up briefly in a nutshell by the kids on the playground analogy "2 kids on a playground playing ball, 1 kid says to the other kid give me your ball and every time you want to play with it I'll charge you a fee also every time you want to let someone else play with it I'll charge you another fee".

The banking system started with gold and silver before anyone knew there was a banking system.

You read about the distinct change from livestock and produce being money to actual gold and silver being money in the Bible way back in the old testament. As you read the book of Deuteronomy chapter 14 verse 23, it talks about tithing and then it went on to describe what tithes were such as corn, wine, oil, herds and flocks; then it explained how if your journey was too long and your destination too far to carry all those things that you should sell those possessions for "money." This is evidence that money was the means in which business transactions were conducted before physical banks.

There are many mediums of exchange; thus, gold and silver have always been universal. It was not until the 15th and 16th centuries during the Roman Empire that the banking system really took off in a literal sense. Back then, the men carried big purses, not the women in those days and the reason why men carried purses was because the purses were full of gold and silver. It was the men that traveled and conducted business, it was the men that went to the marketplace and they would buy things from the merchants with the gold stored in their purses. At the end of the day, the merchants would then take all the gold they bought and carry their heavy purses back to their houses.

Over time, somebody came up with an indigenous plan; he thought to himself, "why don't I come up with gold certificates that way people don't have to carry all that gold"? Why not just allow people to bring their gold to me "The Goldman," with that sinister laugh Bahahaha. So, it is said that the Goldman created a system where he allowed those entering the marketplace to store their gold with him; in return, he would give them gold certificates. These certificates stood for the amount of gold each person deposited with the Goldman so that they could go into the marketplace and did not have to carry around those heavy purses. At the end of the day, week or month, the merchants went to the Goldman with all the certificates he accumulated and receive an equal amount of Gold. Now, he did not have to carry all that gold all over the place while trading and depending on the amount of goods sold on a good day, merchants would have a ton of gold in their purses. They were susceptible to thieves and the like, so taking it to the Goldman was very beneficial to commerce. Here is 100 pieces of gold, Mr. Goldman and here are 100 certificates Mr. Merchant and this went on perfectly for quite some time until like in any business of course, the crook comes into the picture.

He then says to himself, "I'll just convince everyone to recirculate the certificates that way they don't have to worry about the storage if their gold, it's in a safe place."

The people believe him and put their trust in him, so what does he do, he cooks up another scheme to fatten his purse. Since he is a goldsmith, he decides to meltdown all the gold he has on deposit and add cheaper miscellaneous metals and add the gold only on the top layer, keeping for himself many pounds of 100% pure gold bars. When the people came to retrieve their share, he gladly hands them over a pile of fake gold bars.

If that is not bad enough, the crook always finds a new objective to continue to get over. In this instance, the Goldman took advantage of the fact that some people were not coming back to redeem the gold for weeks or months at a time, sometimes longer.

So now he makes up more gold certificates than he has in supply (and even that gold has been watered down) he is basically inflating the supply. So now, more things are purchased with these certificates, but they are not really backed by anything, which is how we got to our financial system.

America was on a gold standard as well in the early 1900s, where the American greenbacks were printed based on the amount of gold we had on reserve. Also, the coins that were in circulation were authentic silver or gold, but what do you know the government decided to stop using that. They figured out the same scheme as was done centuries before paper money came into existence. President Franklin D. Roosevelt in 1933 took America off the gold standard, meaning he legally stopped printing money backed by gold in order to print as much money as he wanted. The dollar use to read "pay to the bearer upon demand," but the law Roosevelt passed made it illegal for banks to pay out gold to those who looked to redeem it. He also made it illegal for regular citizens to own gold...sounds criminal don't it? Well, welcome to the land of the free.

This is why this country now has an excess of dollars floating around, and its value has decreased tremendously every year since 1933. If you do not believe me just think about it, what did $1 buy you 10, 20, 30 years ago compared to now? I remember back in the 80s I could go to the store with $1 and get a big bag of chips, a pop, some candy and might even have some change left over. I mean yeah, you can still spend $1 but you are going to get a lot less bang for your buck because the value has decreased due to having so many dollars in circulation. This is the basis of supply and demand. The harder it is to obtain something, the more valuable it is. Now, of course, the dollar holds value; the problem is there are trillions of it in circulation, so that has a major effect on the economy, the price of products & services and how much work is needed to achieve something.

Investments are considered cash vehicles because they can take your money from 0 to 100, then arrive at its desired destination when they perform correctly. The higher the rate of return (meaning the faster the vehicle), the wilder the ride (meaning the riskier the investment), so all in all, the greater the risk, the greater the reward.

You should become your own bank and only use retail banks as a conduit. Basically, just use them to interact financially with other accounts & companies. For instance, if I want to transfer money to various trading accounts, pay my bills online, pay people via PayPal, Cash App, etc., order take out or something like that, those are the main reasons I use banks. Sometimes depending on what kinds of business you are involved in or taken care of, you may be needed to give bank statements for the past 90 days or so, like in the case of obtaining a mortgage. So, there is another purpose for a functioning checking account. But to be clear, Retail banks are not cash vehicles where I put my cash thinking it is going to grow in value from massive amounts of interest on my deposits. Banks are just regular companies traded on the stock market, just like any other public company that you may want to invest in. The only difference between them, for example, let's say a company like Apple Inc. is one company that offers products such as iPhones, tablets, computers and the other offers services such as transfers, loans, deposits, withdrawals and custody of your cash.

There are different types of banks that make up the banking system, and they have so many differences between them:

- *Retail Banks*

- *Commercial Banks*

- *Central Banks*

- *Cooperative or Mutual Banks*

- *Investment Banks*

- *Private Banks*

- *Online Banks*

- *Credit Unions*

Retail Banks, Commercial Banks and Investment Banks are the main three types of banks that the average person will likely do business within the course of their lifetime. JP Morgan Chase, Bank of America, Fifth Third Bank are publicly traded companies that offer stock to the world, just like any other company. They report earnings every quarter just like any other company; they must show every detail of how they run their activities. In fact, if you wanted to start your own bank, you could learn how to run it by investing and studying how they carry out their day-day activities.

Retail Banks

When you drive through the streets in inner cities on the main roads, all you see is *Retail banks* such as National Bank, Wells Fargo, etc. all these are Retail banks and they have certain regulations that dictate how they do business. They mainly deal with the average worker and small community businesses meaning this is where most people cash their checks, hold standard checking & savings accounts, safe deposit boxes and where most businesses bring their deposits (money they made for the day). This is why you have probably seen Armored trucks pulling up once or twice. Go inside and tell them you want to invest in the stock market because you want to own shares of Nike or Walmart. They are going to show you all the mutual funds they offer, which are a basket of various stocks, ETFs, and index funds (further discussed in chapter 3). Most of those bankers do not even have a series 7 licensed to also be able to offer stocks to their customers so they can only offer you mutual funds. What that basically means is give us your money, and we'll invest it for you into a basket of different stocks in which companies have already given us premiums for offering it to our customers or we invested in these companies years ago and now want to unload our shares to you. So, it is more beneficial for them to offer these mutual funds to you than it is for you to profit off the individual stocks on your own.

Commercial Banks

These types of banks are like Retail banks as they offer deposits, checking & savings accounts, CD's (Certificate of Deposit) and loans. However, these loans are more geared towards businesses rather than the average person. These banks include Citibank, HSBC Bank, Santander Bank and Royal Bank of Canada.

Investment Banks

Edward Jones, Fidelity, Charles Schwab, Morgan Stanley, Merrill Lynch, Raymond James, Franklin Templeton, etc. these are investment banks where an average person cannot walk inside and cash a $200 payroll check. You will not see these establishments on every corner of the hood like the retail and commercial banks. These institutions are mostly in suburban areas where rich people live as they are most of their customers.

Central Banks

These banks oversee their nation's commercial banking system, managing the supply of money printed and circulated for that nation or group of nations. They set the interest rates while balancing inflation, all the while affecting things like employment, real estate and corporate expansion positively or negatively.

What is important to know about banks and the United States monetary system is that The Federal Reserve is not a governmental agency nor is it owned or controlled by America, but is a private entity controlled by banking cartels. If you were to go even deeper into global economics, you will see that the entire world banking system is owned by only a few families such as The Rockefellers, The Rothschilds, The Medici family, etc. Do your research; you will see that the world is not controlled by Presidents nor politicians but bankers.

CHAPTER 3

SAVINGS 101

The ability to save is the foundation for every other principal discussed in this book. If you can't fight off those impulses to buy everything you see on T.V., those desires to keep up with the Joneses, those habits of yours that you've been trying to kick for years, those beginning of the year splurges with your income tax returns, etc. then you will never reach your financial goals. Saving is not about how much money you got coming in, but rather, how well you control what is going out. The greatest lie people tell themselves is, "if I made more money, I would have more money," which could not be further from the truth. If you don't believe me just look at the majority of athletes that go broke within 3-4 years after leaving their profession, or those entertainers that stop making hit records, or most of all look at those people that hit the lottery for millions and 2-3 years later their on food stamps. That shows you that income scores the points, but savings wins the game, sprinkle a little investing on top and you can win the championship (i.e., retirement, generational wealth, passive income, residuals, etc.).

Learn how to "go broke with money," this may sound crazy but just think of all the times you had to budget to get through those rough patches. You made sure you had the bare necessities to maintain and you were so busy focusing on survival that you forgot to pay attention to all the extravagant perks you were missing out on. The next time you get a lump sum of money, live like you're trying to recover from a huge loss and instead of treating yourself to that nice juicy steak at that fancy restaurant, just stay at home and make peanut butter and jelly sandwich...

You would if you were broke!!

The definition of saving is different for rich people than it is for broke people. Saving for rich people means investing. They set up an investment for their kids' college fund, they set up an investment for their retirement fund or put away funds here and there for an investment property. Broke people save all their money for this big plan only to go broke all over again. They save all their paychecks to spend it all on a used car but now they don't have any funds to maintain the upkeep, they save for years to accumulate enough money to put a down payment on a home that they can't really afford, or they save thousands of dollars only to go on a trip to return home with a few pictures and a zero account balance. Not to mention broke people will also borrow beyond their means to do these things as well. Always remember, rich people invest their money first and spend the rest while broke people spend their money first and invest the rest.

Financial Fasting

"Is it such a fast that I have chosen? a day for a man to afflict his soul"?

Isaiah 58:5

If someone wants to lose weight, they will do several things such as go on a diet, some people may even go on a fast, others may practice intermittent fasting. Whether they do it for a week, a month or make it a lifestyle, fasting will produce major results. If you want your net worth to accumulate and save money, you will need to fast financially. So, I will explain what I mean by "financial fasting", this is where you deprive yourself of all your wants, of everything imaginable, everything you spend your money on outside of the bare necessities that you need to live.

30, 60, 90 DAY FINANCIAL FAST

- **No Shopping** (besides groceries and toiletries).

- **No Movies** (go online and find free movies through websites or apps).

- **No Eating Out:** All you can have is home-cooked meals or go over family house and eat dinner.

- **No Vacations:** Put all your travels on hold during this period.

- **No Lending Out Money:** Let your family and friends know that you do not have it. Instead, get them a copy of this book to help them with their financial habits; that way hopefully, they will not ask in the future.

- **No Hair Do's or Hair Cuts:** If you cannot do your hair yourself, ask a friend to do the most basic styles for the time being.

- **No Gambling:** You've risked enough of your money over the years I am sure. Faulty spending practices is the same as gambling; only it is with your future.

- **No Manicures or Pedicures:** During this time just keep your nails clean ladies but nothing extra.

- **No Car Wash:** Do it yourself or use the coin wash, seeing that it is inexpensive.

- **No Habits/Addictions:** Addictions are usually something, some person or some place that you cannot live without and unfortunately has mastered you. What is even worse about addictions is that people are never addicted to things that are good for them.

- **No Home Renovations:** Unless your roof is leaking rain into your living room, put off the new roof, windows can wait and absolutely no upgrades.

Only spend up to 10% of what you have saved on "wants" (clothes, jewelry, shoes). Up to 30% of what you have saved on "needs" (apartment, braces, and firearms). Up to 50% of what you have saved on major needs (house, car, surgery, bail money, lawyer, business.) Never and I repeat never spend 100% of your money on anything nor for any reason.

Overlooked Expenses

A. Car maintenance:

Cars often breakdown when you least expect it, usually after a hard winter or a scorching hot summer. You must do regular tune-ups on your vehicle such as oil change, radiator flush, spark plugs, transmission, brake change, in order to get a long life out of your vehicle, as well as prevent unnecessary costly repairs. These repairs will unexpectedly eat up your savings, income tax returns, etc. and put you in the hole because you will not be prepared for the breakdown.

B. Home maintenance:

Ecclesiasticus 29:21 "The chief thing for life is water, and bread, and clothing, and a house to cover shame."

The biggest fears one can have is pulling into their driveway and seeing their house on fire, a window busted out, a door wide open and you go in to find out that you've just lost everything, some of which can't be replaced such as memorabilia, mementos, cash, etc. Your home is your castle, and if your castle is not properly maintained as well as protected, then that could be a recipe for disaster. Drains should be snaked out, gutters must be cleaned out, roof & foundation inspected ever so often, chimney inspected, smoke detectors inspected, carbon monoxide inspected, furnace and hot water tank checked out. Your castle should also be protected at all times, seeing that you store valuables in your home, important documents, expensive clothing etc. There must be an up-to-date security system in place and depending on the neighborhood. You may need a little extra security such as surveillance cameras, dogs, weapons, etc. because when it comes to protecting your assets and family, it is better to have and not need than to need and not have. Which leads me to homeowner's insurance, not only for reasons mentioned above but if someone slips and falls on your steps at your house, you are liable.

C. Health maintenance:

"Know ye not that ye are the temple of God, and that the Spirit of God dwelleth in you"?

1 Corinthians 3:16

All too often, people tend to only focus on their health when they get injured or get sick and a lot of times that is when it's too late. How can we pay more attention to our bank account than we do to our bodies inside and out, especially seeing that our health is what we use to obtain our wealth? Our physical physique should be where we want it or on its way, since our physique plays a major part in our psychological well-being. Internally we should be seeking perfection, no questions asked! Hospital bills will rack up due to various surgical procedures, prescriptions, and ongoing treatments that if not covered by insurance companies, it will cripple you financially.

D. Traffic violations

There are many drivers who from time to time, are guilty of having a "lead foot" and at times, it has cost me. I remember a time I was in an accident where both of us walked away without a scratch but there were deductibles, out-of-pocket repairs, projects held up and premium increases. All of which could have been much worse and more costly especially if there were alcohol involved, no insurance, etc. I have seen people lose their driver's license and force to ride a bus because they didn't think their finances couldn't be affected by traffic. I have seen business owners worth millions sent to prison for driving drunk and causing a vehicular homicide, I've seen people wreck brand new sports cars that they didn't have insurance on but was still stuck with the bill.

You need to have car insurance; you can't be on the road without it because if you hit someone, then you're liable for damages to their vehicle, hospital bills, etc.

You must be your own financial advisor with every turn you make on the road, behave as if each turn is an investment in which you could lose thousands of dollars or even worse, your freedom.

E. Lawsuits

Beware of lawsuits, especially in America being that this is the place where most of the lawsuits are filed (roughly 40 million a year). A country that is home to most licensed attorneys on the planet, armed with enough judicial artillery to destroy even the wealthiest person on earth. This nation's current president Donald Trump has been sued more than 3000 times and last I checked; ALL lawsuits cost money whether you win or lose. In this day and age you cannot look at people because people feel offended if you look at them too hard or even breathe on them. Check the court dockets; there are actual cases of people suing another person somewhere for breathing or sneezing around them (and this is pre-Covid 19).

A woman sued McDonald's because a hot McDonald's coffee burned her, sounds outrageous huh. Well, the jury thought so too because she was awarded millions.

Would you believe that a kidnapper actually sued his victims? How you ask, because they neglected to help him escape authorities, guess they never read the hostage handbook.

In the good ole state Texas, a disgruntled man sued his date because he was offended that she did not give him nor the movie any attention but instead chose to spend the time texting on her phone.

Be careful what you say about people because you can be guilty of libelous for defamation of character and they will sue you. Avoid lawsuits at all costs, they would not only break your bank, but they can destroy you.

F. Relationship management

Manage your relationships like your life depends on it. The relationship you have with yourself first and foremost, the relationship you have with your wife or your significant other. The relationship you have with your kids, with your family, with your co-workers, with your business partners, classmates and even your neighbors, therefore you must manage all relationships. If relationships are not managed, in the worst-case scenario, they are all problems waiting to happen. Think about it; if you do not manage your relationship with your spouse, you can end up in divorce court fighting for half of everything you own, not to mention pieces of your sanity. You must manage the relationship you have with your kids too because a toxic relationship could cause you a lot of headache, heartache and potential pain in the wallet. The closest people to anyone is their neighbors; this relationship is particularly important. Your co-workers may not know where you live, some of your friends may not know where you live, neither your classmates nor even some family members but your neighbors know exactly where you live, when you're home and when you're gone.

Manage the relationship with your neighbors or you could potentially end up in court in a scuffle or some sort of property destruction. The relationship you share with your co-workers may seem easy to manage for some but for others it could be the most dysfunctional. Most of the nation's working population spend more time at their jobs with their co-workers than at home with their families and just like with siblings, arguments and disagreements will occur but losing your job or messing up your income can never be a choice. Unless you are in the 8th grade and a bully, the relationship with your classmates should be the easiest to manage seeing that this environment is one that encourages using your mind intellectually and not carnally. It would be unwise to allow a disagreement or misunderstanding to affect your education, degree or diploma (though it has happened). Not managing relationships with your family could greatly affect you emotionally and it could affect you in times of need.

When you are in need, you may have to depend on them for something and risk them not being there for you.

I saved the most important for last; this is the relationship with Yourself. There are many people who suffer from depression or some mental illness that affects their view of themselves and the life they live. Some suffer from a lack of enthusiasm because they do not love themselves, so they don't do right to themselves. Some suffer from lack of self-worth; some people are not inspired due to so many failures and challenges. Though this book is about never going under money and maintaining other things of value, your self-worth is above all due to it being the most priceless commodity.

Many things can be done to bring peace and happiness into your life, such as listening to motivational audios, being around positive people that make you laugh, children can often brighten up your day. I like to read the Bible or hang out with my family. Various activities can be relaxing to the soul; women should get pedicures and manicures and be pampered every once in a while, (at least once every other month), especially if it does something to a woman's self-esteem. Men should get a massage at least once a month whether they go to see a masseuse or have one come to the house, either way, massages relax the muscles and release stress which takes out some of the pressure from the brain, seeing that men are leaders and providers; therefore they are constantly bombarded with problems and intense situations.

Without the proper release, man or woman could have a nervous breakdown or even worse, many people have folded under the daily pressures of life and decided just to give up. Take the kids on trips, spend time with them doing fun things that make them laugh; they will grow up to be stress-free, outgoing and productive.

CHAPTER 4

HOOD TO WALL STREET

I come from the hood, so my reason for titling this chapter "Hood to Wallstreet" was for my family and friends in the hood who play lottery every day, go to the casinos downtown, throw dice on the corner, play poker and all other forms of gambling. I figured that if you would risk your money doing those things as I have, then the stock market is perfect for you. People have this idea embedded in their heads that you must be some sort of a genius to get involved in the stock market and that could not be further from the truth. I won't use a lot of big words to confuse you and the words I do use that you may not be familiar with, I will do my best to explain it clearly. What I will do is use various examples and scenarios to help you better understand certain information, some of which may be exaggerated or even comical but the purpose is to offer different perspectives to help you get the big picture.

By the time you finish reading this book, you should be able to go on your computer, open a brokerage account and start trading or investing. I started trading in 2009, with no knowledge of the market at all (I do not recommend anybody do that). One of my homeboys flew me out to Seattle, WA, to get away for a month or so and that experience changed my life. He would have poker night every Thursday and all his friends would come over to gamble. Mind you, my homeboy was a design engineer for Boeing (The airplane manufacturer) and his friends were either co-workers or they were professionals in other fields. I would overhear them talking about the stocks they bought and how much money they have made or the real estate revenue they've made from rental properties. I was in a desperate situation and I needed to make some money fast (never do anything out of desperation), so I looked into taking a stock class. Here I am in Seattle, WA, on vacation and my homeboy took me to a Master Builder seminar where they were offering classes starting at $10,000 and that was the half-off price. I did not have that kind of money at the time but even if I did, I wasn't about to spend that amount on learning anything! Once I got back home, I decided why spend thousands on learning the stock market only to turn around and take more money to invest in the stock market, so I just took $4000 and put it in the market. It took me about three weeks to lose every penny, which prompts me to take another $3000 or $4000 and put in the market. This time I actually made $1000 or $2000 before losing it all again but nevertheless, I lost it all again. After a few months of getting my head cracked, I decided to leave it alone and do something else but I remembered throughout the whole ordeal there were times when I made $800 here $1500 there and I'm talking in the matter of days sometimes hours.

It never occurred to me to just read a book or get some kind of information before I got back in the stock market, I thought to myself "I'm gone learn on my own," and I did at the expense of my entire stash. One day, I remembered the one thing that made me money more often than not, and that was when I invested in stocks right before the company reported earnings. So one day, after going through a major crisis being down on my luck, I called a friend and asked to borrow $300 because I knew Apple Inc. reported earnings the next day and there were rumors about them coming out with some sort of tablet PC (which would later become the iPad). Apple shares were trading at about $190/per share and all I had was $300, so buying one share would not give much of a return unless the stock doubled. I decided to buy an "option contract" for $290 and the next day, Apple shares went up to $200/per share, that's a $10 increase and if I had bought the stock I would have only made $10, but my option contract was now trading at $1000. I made a $700 profit in one day from "options," so I never bought an actual stock again, unless it was a penny stock or for my 401k.

A. TRADING VS. INVESTING

There is a difference between trading and investing when it comes to the stock market, though the only thing that separates the two is basically "time." Trading is generally broken up into three different categories (Day trading; Intra-day trading; and Swing trading).

Day trading: When you buy something today and sell it the same day before the market closes.

The government only allows (3) day trades per week unless you have $25,000 in your account; only then will they consider you a pattern "day trader" (it takes a little more for the IRS to recognize you as a pattern day trader).

Intra-day trading: When you buy something today and then turn right around and sell it within seconds, minutes or hours. (Those trades are most often made for the "Futures" or "Forex" markets which we will get into later).

Swing trading: When you buy something today and sell it tomorrow, a couple of days later or the next week.

Investing is generally broken up into two categories, such as short-term investing and long-term investing.

Short-term investing: When you buy something and hold on to it for less than a year.

Long Term investing: When you buy something and hold on to it for one year or longer. (Uncle Sam has special tax obligations for short-term and long-term capital gains as well).

This chapter is geared towards trading and the actions to take when seeking short-term gains from as many price moves as possible, whether up or down. Those who choose to be more of an investor must simply apply these strategies for a longer period (investors use weekly, monthly and yearly charts vs. traders who use minute and daily charts). Most people in the hood want to be involved in opportunities that will result to instant gratification and that is why we go to the casino, play lottery, gamble in the streets, bet on games, etc. So those are the people that will benefit from this information, others will too after all the second-guessing.

HOMEWORK

Homework is what you must do in order to find the right stock, option, or future to invest in or trade, and secondly, so you will know when to get in and get out of your positions. The better you become at doing your homework, the better your chances are at making a profit because analyzing stocks as well as the market is your strongest asset, it separates the players from the speculators. There are two ways to analyze a company and its stock (technical analysis and fundamental analysis), but first you must understand that the "company" might be a good company but its "stock" can be doing bad and vice versa.

Fundamental analysis: When you study the

health of the "company" by looking at its products and/or services, income statements, balance sheets, prior earnings, management, insider buying or selling, basically any and everything that can affect their growth going forward.

Technical analysis: When you study the "charts" of the prospective company's stock to determine where the "price" will go based on where it came from and how it has behaved in the past at certain levels or certain times of the year (We will get into chart reading later on).

THE STOCK MARKET

When I talk to people about the stock market, they like to communicate as if they know what they are talking about instead of just getting new information. First off, humble yourself because it doesn't matter if you talked briefly to somebody who made thousands of dollars from trading or investing, if you work in a bank, if your job offers 401k, chances are you might be clueless to the basic principles of how this machine we call the stock market actually works. As soon as somebody says, "oh I'm already in the stock market I got an IRA or 401k" I tell them you are not in the stock market; some of your money is but you are not! But that statement is two-fold because I also talk to people who say, "I don't want to get involved in the stock market," but the bad news is you already are. If you

have done any of the following: have a bank account, car note, mortgage, been to prison, shop at major retailers, use credit cards, carry cash or basically get out of bed every morning, then 9 times out of 10 you are and have been in the stock market for quite some time, you just don't reap the benefits.

The U.S. market is made up of three major indices (indexes), which are the Dow Jones, the Nasdaq and the S&P 500. There are other indices, but these are the main three that you will see flash across your TV screen every day. Before getting into the technical jargon about how they came about and what they track, in a nutshell, I'll give this example: Let's compare the stock market to the "sports world," now the three major Sports leagues are the NFL, NBA, and MLB. Now, to get updates on everything that has to do with the sports world, you would watch the sports channels, which would be ESPN, NFL ticket, etc.

Viewing the stock market through the same lens, we will look at the major companies as players such as IBM, Google or Amazon IBM plays for the Dow, Google plays for the Nasdaq and Amazon plays for the S&P. These are the indices those players (companies) play for though these players sometimes switch teams (indices) depending on their stats (earnings, market share, etc.). Watching channels like Bloomberg & CNBC will keep you up to date on which players are winning or losing.

Stocks often move with the indices it trades on, so if your company is listed on the Dow Jones and the

"DOW" is down for the day then there's a strong chance that your company's stock will be down too, the same is true for the Nasdaq and the S&P 500.

Dow Jones: Is made up of the 30 top industrial companies in the U.S., and their performance is compiled to create an average that represents the state/health of the industrial sector. The list includes companies like Boeing, DuPont, ExxonMobil, General Electric, etc.

Nasdaq (National Association of Securities Dealers Automated Quotations): Is the second-largest exchange in the world, with roughly 1.8 billion shares traded daily, mainly by banks, tech companies, penny stocks, amongst others.

S&P 500 (Standards & Poor's): Is made up of 500 of the top U.S. large-cap (Blue Chip) companies totaling trillions of dollars. In order to be added to the list, a company must have a market cap of around 6 billion.

Ticker Symbols

Every stock, option, future, commodity, currency and any other financial product that can be traded on the open market has what's called a "ticker symbol" as an identifier which separates that company, commodity, or financial product from others. Apple Inc. ticker symbol is (AAPL), Ford Motor Company ticker symbol is (F), eBay ticker symbol is (EBAY). Some ticker symbols may be the abbreviated version of that company's name but sometimes the best abbreviation may be taken and a company will be forced to settle for a ticker symbol that doesn't match their name such as United States Steel their ticker symbol is (X) or Southwest Airlines ticker symbol is (LUV). At any rate, these will be the symbols you see flashing across your TV. screen as you watch your favorite stock news channel, you will first see the company name, its ticker symbol, stock price, and then the change for the day in a dollar amount accompanied by a red or green arrow signifying if that stock is up or down for the day.

B. Stocks

Grocery Store Analogy

Let us look at the stock market as if it were a grocery store, so you walk in and every isle is a different sector, isle one Automotive sector, isle two Retail sector, isle three Tech sector. So, you want some Ford stock huh, let us go down isle one; also, you want to pick up some Apple stock, ok let's go down isle three. So, on each shelf, there is a different selection of stocks (companies) to choose from, all you have to do is find the right reasons to buy.

Picking Stocks

First and foremost, do not fall in love with any stock!! Stocks are like "dates" you take them out and if you like them, you date again, if you don't you find something better to date. If you fall in love with a stock there's no more dating because now you're stuck and you got to stick around through all the ups and downs just like in a marriage (now I'm not saying don't get married just let it be with a person, not a stock). Too often, people tell me they want to invest in this company or that company because they think it is going to go up, my reply is when and how do you know? The stock market has economic cycles where certain times within the year, the entire market goes up due to key factors involving the U.S. dollar, commodities, weather, etc. most of which we have no control over. Also, different industries and/or sectors

have cycles and rotations that change from quarter to quarter, example: In the fourth quarter which is the last three months of the year, retailers get a boost in revenue due to the holiday season, now that is just one of many things to take into account when making investment decisions but you can learn all that later because the tools I give in this book are all the things I use to buy and sell stocks, options and futures.

Pick stocks that are about to do something NOW!! Not a year from now or maybe when Trump gets out of office but today, tomorrow or next week at the latest. Companies who are about to report earnings have the greatest chance of making major price moves that you can capitalize on immediately after or sometimes just before. Companies that major investment firms are buying (institutional investors) into because they are the force behind a stock moving up or down, not little ole you and me. Those companies whose stocks are forming "base patterns" on their charts such as "cup-with-handle," "cup-without-handle," "double-bottom," "3-weeks tight," "4-weeks tight," etc.

These are identifiable patterns that show up only during technical analysis of a company's chart.

In this book, we only cover some of the reasons to buy into a particular stock but as your knowledge grows trading with these strategies, you will learn all about P/E Ratios (Price-To-Earnings), EPS (Earnings Per Share), ROE (Return on Equity), SMR rating (Sales+Margins+Return on Equity), EBITDA (Earnings

Before Interest Taxes Depreciation & Amortization), as well as other forms of fundamental analysis.

When & Why Strategies

Knowing "what" stocks to buy or sell is only half the battle; the other half is knowing when to get **in** and why to get **out (entry & exit strategies)**. When and why strategies can only be used with patience and discipline because if you don't have the patience to wait for the entry position, then you won't have the discipline to exit after you've made a profit or taken a loss.

When you enter a trade based on an earnings play, it is important to get in 1 to 3 days before because sometimes the stock may take off in anticipation. But to be on the safe side, I will get in just minutes before the market closes; that way, when your company reports earnings right after the market closes or before the market opens the next day, you are already in.

When entering a trade after it has formed a "base pattern," professionals have determined that you must get in before the stock goes up 5%.

Example: If a stock formed a cup-with-handle and the tip of the handle is formed at $50.00/a share, then you must get into that trade before that stock reaches $52.50 because by then, the stock has already taken off. There may be alternative buying points, but you will learn that as you become more experienced.

Never buy a stock that's "going down" because you think it's going to go back up and never short (sell) a stock that's going up because you think it's going to go down, you want to wait until it goes in the desired direction first, then make your move.

Charts

Charts are the graphs you see with all the up and down lines that show the past or present price movement of a stock. The "line" charts are similar to the heartbeat chart you see in the hospital when someone flatlines and dies, if a stock chart does that, then someone has lost a lot of money. There are also different kinds of charts but some of the most successful trader's use "candlestick" charts.

"Candlestick" charts allow you to spot certain buy and sell signals in an easier way than other charts (in my opinion). You can look at other types of charts just for information purposes but when it is time to put in an order, the most identifiable signals show up on candlestick charts. In this section, we will go over "buy" or "sell" signals that you must wait for to enter or a trade. Though the "stock" or "future" will move up and down without any of these signals appearing, you must be disciplined and wait for them because those moments will present the best opportunities to make profits. Though there are many signals that can be identified on a candlestick chart, we will only deal with these (6) for simplified purposes as well as history showing that these signals in particular have given me my most successful trades thus far.

Buy Signals: The Doji, The Hammer, The Shooting Star, etc.

Sell Signals: The Upside Down Doji, The Inverted Hammer, The Gravestone, etc.

Indicators: Upper indicators goes on the chart such as Bollinger Bands, moving averages, etc. Lower indicators go underneath the chart such as ADX, Stochastics, RSI (Relative Strength Index), etc.

Base Patterns

I will not go into detail about how to spot these base patterns on charts because it could come off as something too difficult to understand, even though it's not. My intention is to explain to you what each pattern is just to get you familiar with them. I would suggest going online and getting a 30-day free trial stock analyst subscription mainly because there are companies that do all the work for you until you learn how to analyze the stocks yourself. Honestly, for $30-$60/a month, I personally would rather let the professionals do all the homework and tell me when stocks are forming a particular base pattern, so all I have to do is decide which one I want to buy or sell.

I don't recommend taking stock tips from T.V. or the internet without doing your homework because companies pay to have certain stocks promoted for various reasons, all of which may not be for your benefit.

When to Take Profits/Cut Losses

1. After stock does what you wanted it to do.
2. After a major run-up before profit taking.
3. When your trade does not go your way. This is extremely important because all too often you will be down a few dollars and convince yourself that your trade will turn around only to watch it fall lower.

Penny Stocks

Any stock trading under $5.00 is considered a penny stock by market standards; I guess those rich dudes on Wall Street made so much money that $5.00 is the equivalent of one cent. Penny stocks have the most potential to make you huge profits with the smallest amount of money invested in a single trade mainly because they are so cheap and you're able to acquire a large number of shares of a particular company.

Crooks know this as well which is why the market is flooded wit tons of pump and dump schemes.

Technical analysis will not do you much good as far as doing your homework on a penny stock, due to the fact that the stocks movement is based on pure speculation only. The company's fundamentals are really all that matters along with other catalysts that will move the stock up or down:

1. Legal battles such as lawsuits on either end
2. USDA or FDA approvals or denials (biopharmaceuticals really take off after positive results from phase 2 or phase 3 trials of a new drug).

3. New patents

4. New products or services offered (USP Unique Selling Point)

5. Mergers or acquisitions (being bought out by a larger company)

Penny stocks trade on Nasdaq, NYSE, AMEX, OTC-BB (over-the-counter bulletin board), Pink Sheets, TSX, and TSX-V. Different exchanges have different listing requirements, so it's wise to stay away from the companies that can't afford to be listed on the Nasdaq or NYSE, I mean after all their penny stocks and that's enough risk as it is. OTCBB and Pink Sheets are so easy to list on you and I can start a company and have our stock trade on them, so you can imagine the pumping and dumping that goes on there. "Pump and dump" scams where crooks list a stock on an exchange like OTCBB or Pink Sheets and put out false news to pump the stock up then after you buy in, they sell out leaving you holding worthless shares of a company that only exist on paper. So, watch out for the free stock pick promotions and do your homework to make sure they are legit, making some money (millions upon millions to be exact), and something is about to happen with them with a desired time frame, call them if you have to. If pharmaceutical companies are doing well, then subscribe to receive a free newsletter that publishes FDA results so you will have a heads up on which companies might pop!

Starting out, it would be best to focus on what is hot, meaning what new industry is in high demand and you will know because most of the stocks in that sector will have the biggest recent gains. Be picky like you would be if you were buying a dream house to live in, do not settle for less; make sure the company meets your criteria.

C. OPTIONS

"Options" are basically coupons attached to a stock so that people who don't want to own or don't have the money to own the actual stock can buy or sell an "option" contract and still take advantage of the price movement of an actual stock. Each "option" contract represents 100 shares of the actual stock.

Example 1: Let's say you see a tow truck riding up the street towing a small car, the tow truck is the actual "stock" and the small car is the "option" contract, if the tow truck goes up a hill then the small car goes up with it and if the tow truck goes down a hill then the small car goes down the hill as well. Now as a trader or investor, you need to make sure your option contract (car) is being towed by the right stock (tow truck), so if you think that tow truck is going up the hill then you would buy a "Call" but if you think that tow truck is going down the hill then you would buy a "Put."

Options contracts are described as "Calls" and "Puts" to identify the purchase you want to make. They each have a "Strike price" and an "Expiration date" attached to them to further identify the purchase you want to make. Lastly, to acquire an option contract, you must pay a premium.

Calls: Give you the right, not the obligation to buy 100 shares of a stock at a certain price (strike price) before a certain date (expiration date).

Puts: Give you the right, not the obligation to sell 100 shares (that you do not own) of a stock at a certain price (strike price) before a certain date (expiration date).

Strike price (buy/sell price): Is the price you are contracted to buy or sell their stock at, no matter what. Meaning if the actual stock goes up to $100 and your (call) option contract has a $50 (strike price) then you have the right to still buy that stock at $50.

Premium: Is the price you pay initially to buy the option contract. 80% of all option contracts are never exercised but are traded away mainly because if people don't have the money to buy one share of a stock in the first place than they definitely don't have the money to buy 100 shares. 10% of all options get exercised meaning the option holder bought or sold the 100 shares at the strike price and the remaining 10% expire worthless because people did not capitalize off them while they had value.

The price (*premium*) you pay for an option contract is made up of intrinsic value and time value, meaning the further the expiration date the more *time value* will be factored into the price and depending on the strike price compared to the current stock price more or less *intrinsic value* will be factored in. So basically if it's April and a stock is trading at $500 and you bought a "June $498 call" for $350 ($3.50 X 100 shares) then there's already $2 worth of *intrinsic value* built into the premium price and the other $1.50 is all *time value* (expectation value so to speak).

That scenario dealt with "calls," meaning you bought the option expecting the stock to go up but in the case of "puts" you will sell it first, sounds confusing right, like how do you sell something you don't own?....Welcome to the stock market! It works just like being a middleman:

Example 2: Aye Mike, you still selling that car? Yeah. How much you want for it? $500 (contract)....Aye Craig, you still looking for a used car? Yeah. I got one for $900. Cool bring it over.... Deal is done and you make $400, the only difference with options is the *premium* you pay for that privilege to obtain contracts, but after that, whatever gain or loss you make is all yours.

CHAPTER 5

CRYPTOCURRENCY/DIGITAL ASSETS

Remember when people used foods stamps to buy food? Now, if you walk into a store with food stamps to pay for your groceries, you will be told they are worthless in paper form because now food stamps come on what is called Bridge cards.

If you put money into a bank account, your banker will give you a debit card to make purchases at various stores around the world. Your spending limit is based on how much you have deposited thus far, give or take some interest but not a dollar more. Food stamps now work the same way.

Cryptocurrency is a new asset class, unlike the others (cash, gold, silver, etc.) since it moves digitally.

What is important to know when dealing with this space is that there has not been a new asset class since the 1700s. If we go back in time to the beginning, it started with the barter system, you know, people traded their livestock such as cattle, chickens, fish, etc. also their fruits, vegetables, wheat and stuff like that before the mining and trading of precious metals.

After many years, they started mining and trading gold, silver, copper and other precious metals as a means of exchange being that these metals served many useful purposes such as building materials, cooking utensils, jewelry, etc. This went on for thousands of years until they developed stock certificates where people would sell pieces of their company in order to get extra money to run or expand their business, then corporate and government bonds, then certificates of deposits (C.O.D.'s) savings bonds, stock options, futures, commodities and of course cash amongst other things. These are asset classes that we all know but now we have entered this new age where value moves as quickly as the speed of light and we call them digital assets.

Cryptocurrency runs on blockchain technology which is very complex in nature but not necessarily needed to be understood to make money. We invest in many things and do not understand all the inner mechanics of how they work because all we need to know is the basics.

Take for instance, this new company Ripple who has a cryptocurrency called XRP; they are considered the

Internet of value. So, if you look at the Internet how it is made up of information passing between companies, institutions, businesses and people every day all over the world. This company Ripple is doing the same thing with money; they've coined themselves as the Internet of value meaning any amount of money in any currency that you want to send or receive, you can do it over their network. As you know, we do this with information over the internet so they just basically digitized value and turned it into information allowing banks and payment providers (Western Union, MoneyGram, etc.) to send, transfer, trade and store money digitally using something called distributed ledger technology (DLT). Meaning if you had a notebook (ledger) names of random people on one side and on the other side of the page has the names of everyone they owe, how much they owe and what country they live in, you can with the click of a button pay everyone (distribution) in every country in their native currency the amount they're owed in the matter of seconds for pennies on the dollar.

Now every company in the crypto space has different blockchain technologies such as Stellar Lumens, Tron and Vechain, to name a few. Vechain is in the business of monitoring the movement of products and services in the supply chain amongst other things. It has created an ecosystem that provides information of the entire lifecycle of a product from start to finish, so when a company receives its shipments of meat or produce, due to supply chain management it has a 360 view of the entire process; like what was the temperature of the vehicle transporting the load and if it went above the maximum temperature allowed.

As we enter this new generation and technology gets a little deeper into artificial intelligence, just know this is the new wave of things. This is where the world is going, everything is becoming digitized, cash is going digitized, information has been digitized but things such as contracts will be tokenized and digitized as well. If I hire a contractor to build my house the deal will be done using smart contracts tied to the company that provides the materials, the city where the permits will be pulled, all that way to the bank that transfers the money, all this can be done using a smartphone.

Real estate will even be digitized; soon, you'll be able to buy pieces of real estate like you're able to buy pieces of a stock or pieces of a company. Some Real estate company or governmental body will divide the value of that property and offer it in a market that you can trade on. Judging by history, once you have heard rumors about it, that means it is already here. Like the rumor which is now a reality that the world is moving towards a cashless society, especially with the new pandemic (Coronavirus) that is assuring that this agenda is phased in a lot quicker. If we're required to practice social distancing with our bodies increasing the fear of touching somebody, you must know that money travels all over the world so just by interacting with people financially in trade with dollars causes a conflict of interest. It is a high probability that a virus can be contracted and passed along through global commerce, so with this; you have accelerated the path to making that rumor come true.

But even with a pandemic the powers that be will still have an uphill battle pushing the cashless society agenda because people (important wealthy people) know how governments operate. Meaning if the government had all that power in their hands and decided to hit the switch on someone's ability to buy so that they can't move like you want to it will be as if they removed half of the freedoms we enjoy.

Think about it in terms of today, if the government locked your bank account up, you could still go and use your cash, but in a cashless society, things would get hectic really quick. You could not buy groceries, clothes, pay your light and gas bill, buy toilet paper, nor the water bill to flush the toilet. Also knowing how sinister governments can get, they could pass laws deeming it fraud and a felony for anyone to transfer to people on their blacklist. These are just some concerns that will hold this process up as well.

Right now, there are around 4000- 5000 different digital currencies in the world though very few of them hold any value meaning very few have utility and purpose in the marketplace. Maybe 1%-5% have real world purpose and a chance at mainstream adoption but the other ones are just trying, or they are scams.

The entire crypto market cap is worth just over 200 and some odd billion dollars. Now if you are looking at your bank account, you are probably like whoa that's

a lot of money. But when you look at it compared to the other asset classes such as gold, its market cap is around 8 trillion dollars; the US stock market cap is $30 trillion dollars. So, the crypto asset space is really a baby on a global scale of things for anybody asking, what is it? So right now, nobody really knows about it and it is a space where things happen very fast. Bitcoin, the first digital asset was established in 2010 selling for pennies and then went to dollars. By 2017 Bitcoin was trading for $20,000 a coin and people were made millionaires overnight. Ethereum is another one that was trading for pennies in 2015 and while I was looking for somewhere to put some cash and never heard of Ethereum which is precisely why in 2017 when the coin went up to $1300, I wasn't a part of that wave of millionaires. Now if this is what a market cap of just a few hundred billion can do, just imagine when this thing gets into the trillions once everybody is made aware of what is going on. Crypto is not a fly by night fad, no its nothing that is going to go away.

You know, back in the day when the internet first came out people were skeptical and did not believe on the internet. Warren Buffett, the famous investor, is quoted saying he did not believe in companies like Google or Amazon. All too often people find it easy to believe in a small company doing something average but find it hard to believe in a nobody company taking over the world. Who would have thought Netflix would put Blockbuster out of business, DVD's would replace VHS tapes or that Streaming would replace DVD's?

All the people that said, "I don't believe in the internet" now guess what, every company has to interact with the internet, every man, woman and child has to interact with the internet, you have no choice. If you are in business or you communicate with somebody that is not in your house, nine times out of 10 you must go through the internet. So, it is one of those things that does not have any competition unless someone harnesses the power of mental telepathy.

The only thing that is holding Crypto up from taking off to the moon is government regulations, US government regulation to be exact, seeing that most of the other countries are already on board. The US government being the world's superpower, is pondering a little further than just regulation. They are thinking "How can we make the most money"? How can we control it? It is this procrastination on the part of the politicians that is really holding the big boys up from pouring all their money into it.

Big boys meaning the Goldman Sacs, Institutional investors, hedge fund managers these are the entities who control the world's retirement accounts, pensions, 401k's and most of the wealthy individual's money. Once the regulation is clear on what crypto is, what's a commodity and what's not, that's when it will be too late for any early investors because prices will skyrocket overnight. There will not be another opportunity to make money like this again in our lifetime that's for sure if it will ever be again because it's an opportunity of a lifetime for this generation. Just like it was in the 1990's during the Dot.com boom in the middle of the internet era. Just like it was in the early 1900s during the industrial revolution era.

Also, by the industry being digital, you got to watch out for hackers, you know. Think about it when you buy a stock, you do not get a certificate in the mail, it's stored on an exchange that's regulated. Cryptocurrencies right now carry some unforeseen risks reason being that these new exchanges are prone to seasoned hackers. Also a lot of times, the way the process is set up by people sending their crypto to various wallets and addresses, if you lose your key or you send it to the wrong address for whatever reason...you lose your crypto for good. It is a whole lot of Bitcoin that's lost forever (hundreds of millions of dollars) because of the communication process and how you got to put a whole bunch of numbers to send to an address. And if you miss one number and send that Bitcoin to that address is gone forever. Worse yet hackers can hack in and take your stuff, so you got to protect it. A lot of people protect their crypto on external sources such as hard wallets, USB drives or offline computers but all your information and money is stored on that all and you keep it outside the internet locked up in your safe, safe deposit box or something like that. Cryptocurrency is a new medium of exchange, right now you cannot buy crypto like how you buy stock on E*TRADE, Ameritrade and Fidelity.

Some common name brokerages offer crypto purchases like Robin Hood and Cash App but the two major crypto exchanges are Binance US, and Coinbase those are the two that I use, there are others but I haven't done any business with them so I can't tell you about them. Coinbase allows you to link your bank accounts up and begin trading once verified though with Binance US you can buy crypto directly with your debit card. I have both because some cryptos can't be bought on Coinbase due to them not being listed yet, but you can buy others on

Binance so when this thing takes off like I'm expecting it to, you won't be left out.

I don't want to be left out of the party, but you should also know that I don't invest all my money in crypto, but is a nice amount of whatever I make so that I'm positioned to take advantage of a nice move. A nice 5000%- 6,000% move to the upside would be very helpful that way in a couple of years I can retire. There are some cryptocurrencies that are up 30,000% - 60,000%, Bitcoin is trading over $9000. Then you got some cryptocurrencies that are trading under a penny. I mean, isn't that ridiculous for an asset to be under a penny? If it goes up, if it doubles in value, and it goes to a penny, a penny and a half, you have doubled your money. That is crazy, to sit on an investment like that and wait for it to go to $1, is that far-fetched? I do not think so.

CHAPTER 6

TAXES

"And Jesus answering said unto them, Render to Caesar the things that are Caesar's, and to God the things that are God's. And they marveled at him".

Mark 12:17

As long as power has existed, there has been "taxes," King Solomon the richest king that ever lived, was paid taxes by all nations.

In this day and age, governments have found a way to tax everything down to the water you drink, even the air that you breathe, they tax you coming into this world and they tax you going out. Much more than just applying tax to a product, service, commodity, monies earned, etc. taxes are applied multiple times throughout each cycle. Take a pair of Jordan's for instance, once the shipment of shoes enters the country, Mike must pay import taxes, duty taxes, tariffs, etc. Then he must pay a shipping company to transport all those shoes to various stores throughout the country by truck, train and/or air all the while those shipping costs will incur taxes. After those shoes hit each desired location and a few hours have passed, everyone will have purchased every pair of fresh crispy Airs in the store. Now the great phenomenon about this is Uncle Sam will make his money even before Michael Jordan by taxing those sneakers multiple times as they enter the country through the ports all the way down to the taxing of every sale of every shoe at the cash registers. Wow, once Big Mike sells the entire shipment of those shoes, Uncle Sam will want to know how much money he made in revenue so that he can of course, charge him the proper taxes on those hefty profits. Afterwards, if Mike decides to keep the rest of his profits in some account where it grows interest, then you know who will come knocking again for his cut of what the government calls capital gains tax. Capital gains taxes are applied to your money when it makes money, meaning profits from investments which is taxed differently from wages that you earn from working a 9-5 job.

There are several categories of taxes such as: Income tax, Payroll tax, Property tax, Consumption tax, Tariff (taxes on international trade), Capitation (a fixed tax charged per person), Fees and tolls, Business tax capital gains tax, Income taxes, Death tax, Luxury tax and many other taxes making tax law the most confusing of all areas of law. We will deal with the most common tax situations that many of us will encounter but I encourage you to do some research on the different categories on your own more in-depth as it pertains to your individual situations. Also, I encourage people (especially entrepreneurs) to do their own individual taxes, Business Tax and/or Personal Taxes.

Learning to do your own Taxes, Business Tax, Personal Taxes will benefit you in the long run and even if you hired a professional, you would have some idea of what is going on with your finances. It makes you more conscious of your spending habits as well so that by year-end, you would have intentionally done all the necessary things to ensure you owe less or get a greater return. There are many easy to use software programs that will walk you through each step one by one (some free, most cost under $200) thus simplifying the process for a complete novice.

Every year you have the people that are hoping for a large income tax refund and then you have the wealthy, entrepreneurs and businesses owners hoping for a large tax break. It's important to know that rich people (typically) do not get back any returns due to them making a lot of money and no tax being taken out; therefore, they didn't overpay the IRS, which is how us little people receive a refund in the first place from overpayment throughout the year.

In this chapter, we will deal with taxes as it pertains to you personally, as well as in your business. It is quite common for people to start LLC's (Limited Liability Companies) for tax purposes first and business purposes second, then there's other reasons such as extra income purposes, etc. though there are many reasons why an LLC is needed. Think about how often throughout the year you spent thousands of dollars on fixing up your car, buying a house, fixing your house up doing minor or major repairs, maybe you took a couple of business trips. All that activity is potentially tax-deductible (tax write-off) and the government gives you credits for the money you spend in your business, the parts of your house that you use for your office, your car, your travel, your gas or mileage, all of these things can be written off. The rule of thumb is not to give Uncle Sam more than he is supposed to get but instead keep that money throughout the year and invest it to make profits. Also, rich people are professionals at limiting the amount of tax liability on those profits by the money that they spend and the credits that they receive. Now, this is not tax advice. Please, by all means consult a tax professional. I am just telling you that over the past ten years I've done my own taxes, I've hired people to do my taxes, I've even been audited which is not the most exciting experience. I cannot stress enough the importance of keeping your receipts because without them, you cannot prove that you made certain purchases. Now some people might be thinking "well I use my debit or credit card so I can just print out my transaction history." Rightfully so but you must understand that bank statements only show the amount spent, date and company name but it does not show what was bought. During an audit, the IRS will want to see bank statements, receipts as well as your company's record book which should all add up one with the other. If you keep proper records, an IRS audit is nothing more than an irritating inspection of financial practices.

Something many people do not know is that you can hire your kids for your business, put them on payroll and write them separately from the earned income credit. Once again, speak to a tax professional about this because it is a great benefit to write off all the money you give them just cause or for an allowance or buying them stuff, sending them on trips, whatever when they can work for it and that money can be written off. It is a business expense because they will be your employees.

Some people might have vehicles in their backyard maybe it runs a little, maybe not and but either way you could donate those vehicles to charity and receive a charitable tax deduction. Property taxes, you know, sales taxes and all those taxes will tax-deductible, even the amount you pay your CPA or your tax professional to prepare your taxes are tax-deductible.

CHAPTER 7

THE REAL ESTATE

"The chief thing for life is water, and bread, and clothing,
and an house to cover shame".

Ecclesiasticus 29:21

G etting a mortgage is not buying a house no more than financing a vehicle is buying a car though real estate is a must; it is by far one of the best investments I have ever made. It's an asset that you don't really have a choice to have in some form or fashion because you must have a roof over your head whether you're paying a mortgage, renting or have a land contract. There are many things out here people can choose to own such as an iPhone, they can choose to purchase a Corvette, buy a diamond ring but it's a must that everybody has somewhere to lay their head. Real Estate is one of the most productive ways to generate passive income, meaning buy a property, rent it out and make money hand over first for the rest of your life. Some people work at a job where all they want to do is quit. They may want to get into real estate but never do so. If this is the case for you, try thinking about how much you make a year and divide that by let's say $700 a month rent. $700 x 7 =$49,000 so if you currently make $50k a year you would need seven properties to replace your income. If you trim your lifestyle and adjust how you spend you may be able to get away with

4-5 properties seeing that you will have the extra time to do odd work on the side to supplement.

Passive income is a sure way to stay off the poverty list, also do your research, you will find that 70% of all the wealthy people pass through real estate.

Private lenders

When the bank denies you that mortgage you were hoping for, there are several alternatives at your disposal one being private money lenders. They specialize in funding real estate deals whether it is the purchase price, the rehab budget or both. Private investors will take on this risk as long as the numbers make sense such as appraised value, after repair value (ARV), rehab needed, etc. the property will be the surety which allows for a less stringent approval process compared to banks.

Hard money lenders

Hard money is the same as private money in the sense that the money is from a private investor as well as the process differing from traditional banks but the conditions of the loan are structured a bit different involving points, percentages, variations in the length of loan, etc.

Wholesaling

This method of buying and selling properties are becoming increasingly popular amongst new investors entering the world of real estate due to the ease of operations and the absence of the need to acquire any license. This is where the $0 down method comes into play where you can make money off deals without having any skin in the game. Wholesalers draw up contracts with motivated sellers to buy their property at a predetermined amount only that they don't actually buy the property, what happens is the wholesaler then takes that contract and sells it to a motivated buyer for a higher amount thus pocketing the difference. These deals of course, are done in reverse and depending on the situation, contracts could be assigned to multiple people to get the deal done with assignment fees are divided amongst all parties involved. Contracts can also be drawn up to purchase property subject to foreclosure thus circumventing the process even if the property has already been foreclosed on and the owner has moved on depending on the timeframe, money still can be made on that property.

I have bought properties and turned right around and sold them in a matter of days. I have bought properties for pennies on the dollar to fix them up in order to rent them out for monthly profit. The fix and flip method is a good method for people who know how to work on properties themselves or have friends and family that works on properties. Maybe you know where to find good deals on materials so you purchase a property for let's say $20,000 put $20,000 into it then sell it for $75,000…that could get a little addictive the more you do it. Investors who take advantage of the do-it-yourself method (D.Y.I.), the cheaper the repair costs will be and these days you can look on YouTube and find out how to do just about anything. I just finished gutting an entire rental property, just to learn how to put it back together again. I plan on living in it just for a little bit, sell the one that I am living in currently and then do it all over again. I remember me and a partner of mine had purchased like several properties and after we had like 7 or 8 at once we had one guy working on maybe three or four of them. It turned out that he also wanted to get into real estate so after he told me how much he wanted to repair my properties I ended up doing a deal with him where I didn't spend a dime on repairs for my other properties. The deal worked out where he paid me a few thousand on top of doing the repairs and I gave him a property free and clear. That had to be one of the most unique deals I have done in real estate, but I've heard of deals even more creative than that one.

I remember doing short sales for my family and my friends years ago when the economy tanked, and my mother had a property where she owed over $100,000. When I told her, I was going to do a short sale on her house she was afraid mainly because she did not understand the process as most people don't. Once I told her to stop paying her mortgage she got interested, she stopped paying her mortgage and saved her money. We put the proper paperwork in and six months later the bank sold her house for a little over $20,000 while being forced to forgive her of the remaining balance left over. I then took the money she saved up along with some money she had in the bank and bought her a house free and clear. Now the IRS looks at the amount forgiven as income, but I showed her how to file the necessary documents with the IRS to where that debt would be forgiven. I tried to help others also but they were convinced that it was a scam which reminded me of quote from Harriet Tubman, "I freed a thousand slaves I could have freed a thousand more if only they knew they were slaves".

Fix & Flip

You can buy materials online for dirt cheap, acquire double wall ovens only a year old worth $2000 retail for a couple hundred dollars, $50 marble for your bathroom floor, boxes and boxes of ceramic tile for pennies on the dollar. I did a whole bathroom for what would have cost someone else $6000-$7000 but only cost me $600-$700. You can look on Craigslist, Facebook marketplace, call your local Habitat for Humanity, local resale shops, etc. and find things you need. What you will find in your search is how people give stuff away all the time they just need you to come pick it up. When your mind is on fixing and flipping you have more control over your business and sometimes more control over profit versus investing in the stock market. The difference is you have to wait on that company to see their performance, if your invested in gold you have to wait and see how global economics will play out and the same with commodities such as oil. Now in real estate outside of the general market, you really have more control over what kind of profit you trying to make based on your criteria. I encourage people to get in groups, brothers, cousins, coworkers, business partners and pool monies together to buy properties which will make repair costs a lot cheaper. Spread the capital, resources and work out two or three ways and the sky is the limit to what you can accomplish.

First rule I learned in real estate is the three L's, location, location, location which will in the long run always prove true. Now I have had properties in good locations to where everybody wanted to either purchase or rent and I've also had nice properties in neighborhoods where I couldn't pay a tenant to live in. So always remember, when buying a house to flip it, location is key meaning make sure there aren't many abandon house nearby (which is hard to do in Detroit), make sure there are schools nearby, make sure companies are opening more businesses than they are closing down. Also if you're going to make this a business or a hobby you're going to want to build your Rolodex with plumbers, electricians, painters, drywall finishers, concrete masons, roofers, window installers, etc. because these people will come in handy and could mean the difference of you waiting three months to twelve months to finish a project, spending hundreds of dollars or thousands of dollars due to you only knowing one electrician that is too busy to get the job done. Now you got to go and try to meet someone new, find out if their work is good, if their reliable, not a crook. The worst thing you can do is have a house wired the wrong way and then put all the drywall up so when the inspector comes out and says it's all wrong you'll be forced to tear everything down and start all over again. I have seen this happen and it will slow you down, slow your money down, and worse-case scenario could destroy you.

CHAPTER 8

INVESTING IN YOURSELF

"Ye have sown much, and bring in little; ye eat, but ye have not enough; ye drink, but ye are not filled with drink; ye clothe you, but there is none warm; and he that earneth wages earneth wages to put it into a bag with holes".

Haggai 1:6

The word JOB is an acronym for "**J**ust **O**ver **B**roke. There are overwhelming statistics on how the average person who works a 9 to 5 is one check away from poverty and how most have under $1000 in their bank account. Now I am not saying there's something wrong with working if it is a means to an end, but most people work for 30-40 years only to retire with nothing but a destroyed body full of aches and pains. I feel people should work so they can take the money they make and invest it into a business or some cash vehicle (stocks, crypto, etc.) in order to eventually quit their job and work for themselves. People who study the Bible and follow the ways of Jesus Christ must understand that Christ didn't work for anyone nor did many of his disciples work for anybody but they had their own businesses like for instance, Christ was a carpenter, Peter & Andrew were fishermen, Luke was a doctor and Paul was a tentmaker amongst other things.

I'm not a big advocate of school for the entrepreneurial spirit, not that I'm against school, but school doesn't teach you how to run a business, school doesn't teach you how to be entrepreneur nor does school teach you how to be an investor. School does not teach you how global economics work, it doesn't teach you basic economics to say the least, nor where you fit into the grand scheme of things. School is merely memorization and regurgitation for example, the teacher tells you on

Monday that Christopher Columbus discovered America then comes the test on Friday and the first question reads who discovered America? This isn't learning at all just memorizing and later on in life you find out Christopher Columbus didn't discover anything so not only was those classes a waste of time, but they lied to you with the fake history and false theories. So when it's all said and done school gives you just enough education to where you can pass some tests, graduate with a diploma or degree, get a job, get a car note, get a mortgage now your locked into the American dream. Oh but don't forget now you got to pay back the student loans, you got to pay your car note every month, you got to pay your insurance every month, you have to pay for maintenance on that vehicle, you got to pay your house note. Right? So now your locked in, you cannot miss too many days of work and you can't do anything on the side.

Do you have a job? Is it a good job and are you comfortable with your life? Most people hate their job and they want to quit no matter how good it is. If this is how you feel, then it is a must that you develop a plan and strategy to eventually fire your boss! In the implementation of your strategy, you cannot be somebody that gets their bonuses and blow it, somebody that gets extra money, side money or unexpected money all the time but can't follow a savings plan. You must develop investment plans; you must have multiple savings plans, otherwise, you are going to be stuck in that dead-end job for the rest of your life, unhappy!

You got to have drive and desire. A lot of people will say they hate their jobs but in all actuality are not doing anything to quit. Just wanting to quit isn't enough if it is not matched by an equal amount of drive to do the things that you need to do to get yourself out of that situation.

The money you make should be your ticket out of that dead-end job. Every dollar you set aside or invest should move you one step closer to getting out of the rat race; after all, the whole purpose of these principles is to make your money work for you, not the other way around.

Think of the job you have for a moment but let us reverse the roles a bit, imagine yourself as the boss. Now imagine all your co-workers as your employees then ask yourself, would you allow them to just sit down all day every day do nothing? If your answer is no, then why are you allowing that to happen with your money, especially since you are the boss of your own destiny and your dollars are your employees?

Most people put their money in a bank or under the mattress out of fear of losing it basically saying, "my money don't have to do any work," If you invest it, and you lose a couple of dollars so what it's like the business analogy and a couple of employees quit, so you lost a couple of employees okay now the remaining employees must work harder or you just hire some more. After you get more employees to finish running your business, continue running your life and your finances just as companies run their business, and you will be alright.

People work 8-12hrs every day for someone else, stash their savings in banks owned by someone else, spend their wages at stores owned by someone else, though for some odd reason people refuse to invest in themselves. If the stock market is too much for you to learn, invest in yourself. If banking is too much to learn then why not turn your savings or paychecks into capital and fund your own talents and/or dreams. Do not try to convince people of your dream, if they don't hear you the first time, keep it moving.

When I was a kid, I shoveled snow up and down the street wearing two pair of socks and gloves in the freezing cold.

I pumped gas at the local gas stations and if people said no because they did not have money, I pumped their gas for free. I found out that if they saw me again pumping gas, they would not only let me pump their gas but also pay me for the previous time.

When I was around 12 years old, I use to sell bikes and parts out of my mother's garage and charge kids to fix their bikes for chump change (do not ask me where I got the bikes).

During my teens, I taught myself how to cut hair which saved me from having to go to a barber and also kept some duckets in my pocket cutting all my friend's hair in high school and in college (the short time I was there).

In my early 20s as an artist, I sold paintings and prints in art galleries for hundreds of dollars, the highest painting sold for around $2000.

In my late 20s, I started a clothing line where I painted custom t-shirts out of a local clothing store owned by a guy named Mook. He would take me to New York and Chicago with him teaching me the clothing business. I even did custom painted t-shirts for celebrities such as 50 Cent, Soulja Boy, R-Kelly, etc.

I jumped into real estate after the market tanked in 2008, buying properties for $1000-$2000 renting them out to friends, family and associates. I once bought a fixer upper for $2500, which needed very little work, I rented it out for a couple of years and quadrupled my investment, that showed me real estate was the move. Statistics show that 70%-90% of millionaires have gained a large portion of their wealth from real estate investments.

I forced all my family to give me their money and I bought properties for them for prices ranging from $2500-$6000, which are now worth $20,000-$40,000. I got my mother out of a $150,000 mortgage by making a short sale where she did not have to spend a dime out of her pocket. She pulled a few thousand out of her 401k and bought an investment property for $6000, after she passed that property is one that I now own in a neighborhood where properties are selling for $40,000 - $50,000. Now of course, these are not Rockefeller prices but hey interest is interest.

I designed and manufactured a boardgame called "FAMOUS" ™ which is intended to educate the masses through entertainment about the ups and downs of becoming famous in various professions such as acting, directing, writing, producing, performing and designing.

Running an LLC

While in the middle of writing this chapter, I literally just got a call from a client wanting to start an LLC in hopes that he can take advantage of a government grant being afforded due to the recent pandemic. I am a firm believer that every aspiring entrepreneur should have an LLC, especially with all the various aid programs set up by the government, states, cities and non-profit organizations. As I write this book, the government has been giving out grants and loans to small businesses. You type in your information, fill out the application for your business including bank info and in a few days or weeks later you get a couple thousand in your account and I think it's based on a certain amount of money per employee. Just the benefits of owning a business, as the saying goes "you got to be in it to win it". Many people have small businesses but are yet to incorporate so they cannot take advantage of all the opportunities available. In most states, the process to start an LLC is as difficult as filing a one-page document accompanied by a fee. Some wholesalers will not even allow you to buy their products at wholesale prices if you have not registered your company as an LLC, corporation, partnership, etc. and obtained an EIN (Tax I.D. number).

LLC's are called limited liability companies for a reason because it limits your liability, essentially separating your personal assets and income from your business assets and revenue.

Meaning if someone slips and falls on the steps at your home in your name, they can sue you personally. But if your house is not in your name and instead in your business name, then they would have to sue your company. Meaning all your personal assets that are in your name are protected (of course this is not legal advice, consult an attorney).

So now you know that the LLC was created in case the company does something and somebody sues the company, they cannot take everything you have. Otherwise, they could be entitled to your personal bank account, income taxes and wages if you worked a day job, so that added layer of protection is one of the few gifts from the government. Small businesses are the lifeblood of the economy as they create two-thirds of America's jobs. I know people who cannot get loans or any line of credit because their credit report is shot in their personal lives, but their business can get a line of credit or loan because they're two separate entities. Over the years, I've started multiple businesses all by myself, I only hired an attorney once due to it being a corporation with another person and there were complex terms, stock certificates and others involved that were contractually requiring payment in stock options. I usually just file the documents myself instead of paying thousands of dollars to do something that takes 10 minutes' worth of work. In Michigan, I go to the state website, print out the documents (Articles of Organization), spend $50 and I have a company, next I go on the IRS website fill out the proper form (SS-4) get my tax I.D., go to the bank open up a business account now I'm in business. It's that simple or you can go through an attorney and let them charge you upwards of 1500 dollars.

Investments Overall

"And said he that had received five talents came and brought other five talents, saying, Lord, thou deliveredst unto me five talents: behold, I have gained beside them five talents more".

Matthew 25:20

At the end of the day, there are many things to invest in and resell at a higher price either because time will make it increase in value or you buy it wholesale and resell it for a higher price. The thing is we must always keep our cash flipping in and out of investments compounding profits, whether small or large, it is the secret to wealth building. Albert Einstein, the famous genius once said, "Compound interest is the eighth wonder of the world. He who understands it earns it; he who doesn't pays it." So basically, compounded interest is "interest on interest" or as it relates to investing "profits on profits."

What's important is you know the difference between *Assets & Liabilities.*

Assets are things that make you money, such as your rental property, taxicab, vending machines.

Liabilities are things that cost you money (weekly, monthly, yearly), such as your home, car, boat, beggars.

Once you open your mind to the wide world of investing the list is unlimited of places to put your money. Here are some things I can think of off the top of my head:

- Stocks

- Options

- Cryptocurrency

- Bonds

- Index Funds

- Mutual Funds

- ETF's (Exchange Traded Funds)

- Coins

- Gold

- Silver

- Vintage Art

- T-shirts

- Fashion Accessories

- Water

- Gatorade

- Fruit

- Food

- Vitamins

- Life Insurance

- Scented Candles

- Rental Properties

- Fix & Flip Properties

- Wholesaling Real Estate

between you filling out an application for a job or just getting hired without ever having an interview.

You have got to have connections; you've got to build up your Rolodex because who you know can make a significant difference in your life. It can make a difference between you being rich or you being poor, you living in a mansion or you living on the streets eating out of a trash can. There have been many times where the people I knew got me into places that I couldn't get to myself. I remember when I was doing clothes after I started a clothing line. I was doing custom hand-painted t-shirts (one of the kinds of originals). I was selling them around my city and on consignment in some stores, but it got to a point where I had to go up on my prices, but people did not want to pay. So at that time, I was signed to an independent record company and was friends with some models from my videos that had connections in the industry. After coming up with a strategic plan to take my brand nationwide, I decided to hire a few models as business representatives.

One young lady, had received a lot of attention after being in one of my music videos that she began to star in videos for major artists in the industry. She also got hired on local video shows interviewing stars, so I knew she had a lot of connections. One day I decided to take her out to lunch and tell her the plan I had and that luncheon I explained to her how I wanted to temporarily stop doing shirts locally and only do shirts for stars (Big stars). I figured I would build up my portfolio so that way when I go back to the stores (that turned me down), speak to potential investors or continue making shirts in the hood people would respect my company as a luxury brand and wouldn't have a problem paying me what I wanted. She agreed and said she had a connection with someone at Def Jam and she agreed to set something up. At the time Jay-Z was the CEO, so I painted a shirt of him to possibly give to him for a promo pic in return. I laced her with a few more to display and flew her to New York a week later and did not hear from her for like 5-6 days (I thought something happened to her), then she finally called me. In a low speaking tone, she explained how the Def Jam plug fell through, but she met up with another connection and how I would never guess whose office she was in. I responded who? Though hearing familiar voices in the background saying things like "can he do this or can he do that," it kind of sounded like….nah couldn't be, until she stated, "I'm in the G-Unit office in Manhattan and 50 cent just gave me all this international currency he made on tour. He wants you to put it all on a shirt with his picture". I'm like hell yeah, I can do that when you flying back in? Then I heard other familiar voices seeming to like my designs as well. About a week later, I finished the custom hand-painted t-shirt for one of the most successful rappers in music history and drove up to New York (myself & my business rep), I walked into 50 Cent's office and met with him. Unfortunately, traffic in Manhattan took hours and destroyed any chance of a lengthy visit, but nevertheless, I was grateful for the one I had.

One summer I flew out to Las Vegas for their annual fashion convention "Magic" and once again my business rep had connections that allowed me to communicate with people such as Nick Cannon, the late Kimbo Slice, famous comedians, actors, etc. NBA players were calling my phone wanting to speak to my business rep (did I mention I only dealt with models). There were businesspeople talking about flying me out to Germany to do murals as well as other opportunities.

I made connections from all around the country and even ran into the hottest young up and coming rapper at the time Soulja Boy. He took an interest in my

business rep which got us to pass any security to speak with him; I showed him my portfolio including the work I had done for 50 Cent who was like his mentor at the time and he agreed to allow me to paint him a one of a kind original tee. I flew her out to Atlanta to his home to give him the shirt and he allowed her to come mainly because she was a beautiful woman and she had a unique look so much so that everywhere we went, people were drawn to her. Certain people will have connections that will allow you to get into places that you would not ordinarily get yourself into on your own merits.

I had another female model that was a business rep of mine and she had a few connections as well and she explained how she was friends with a Chicago R&B artist named Rubie Cristyle. I told her to set it up so I can paint a shirt for Rubie Cristyle and R. Kelly while they were on the Double Up tour headed for Detroit. I did both shirts but the day they were to arrive in Detroit I was forced to go to Cleveland, Ohio to open up for a major rapper from Atlanta due to the obligations I had to an independent record company I was signed to at the time. I never got a chance to link up with Rubie Cristyle nor R. Kelly, but my business rep went on their tour bus and gave them the shirts. Unfortunately, her camera malfunctioned and she never got a pic of R. Kelly's shirt (arguably my best work).

I know a guy that owns BB's Diner a well-known restaurant in Detroit and he respected my hustle coming up on 7 mile, so he allowed me to put my painting in his establishment to promote my new art business Platinum Pictures. I had a lot of money pieces of different denominations I accumulated over time so and decided to incorporate it all into the painting. After placing the artwork in BB's restaurant about a week or two later, he called me and said somebody wanted to talk to me about buying my painting. I'm like naw BB that's just for promotional purpose; I want to keep that one. Now in my mind, I'm thinking maybe the guy is trying to give me $100 or something, especially since I had never sold any paintings up until that time. In an attempt to run off the potential buyer I told BB to tell the guy that I wanted a couple thousand dollars, thinking that he would just hang up and I wouldn't have to worry about it anymore, the guy actually said come up here right now and get the money. I drove up to the restaurant's as fast as I could and when I got there, the guy was waiting. He did not ask any questions he just counted out a couple thousand on the table, took the painting and left. I looked at BB like how much you want out of this and without hesitation he said, "man you straight, get your money," Till this day, I still got a long-lasting relationship with him BB and it was that connection that allowed me to make a couple thousand dollars from one painting that only took some hours to do.

Championship Team

*Two are better than one; because they have a good
reward for their labour.*

Ecclesiastes 4:9

Your Championship Team should have a starting 5 of
all-stars:

1. You

2. Tech Wiz

3. The Hustler (Go Getter)

4. The Numbers Guy

5. The Lincoln Lawyer (Attorney)

Outsourcing:

A. Outsource overseas

B. Outsource out of state

C. Your team may be made up of people you don't even know personally.

Analogy: I once knew A Man who knew no one, no one knew him; they both knew each other...no wonder these three got rich, their focus was the team.

When it comes to a dream, you must build a team to bring that dream to life and after you have built that team, don't let anything come in between (you are not going to believe me, but I was not trying to rhyme).

CHAPTER 9

NEGOTIATIONS

"Or what king, going to make war against another king,
sitteth not down first, and consulteth whether he be able
with ten thousand to meet him that cometh against him with
twenty thousand"?

Luke 14:31

No matter how stern a buyer or seller may look, nobody looks sterner than Ben Franklin, the man on the $100 dollar bill.

Negotiations, negotiations, there is an art to negotiations and most people don't know it. The people that do, they make money just by knowing how this game works. There are certain unspoken rules to negotiating that cannot be explained using words nor demonstration, these rules must be developed in the field buying and selling different products and services, with different people, from different nationalities and under a variety of circumstances.

Have you ever ridden past somebody's house and in the driveway, you see a car with a for sale sign in the window? The for-sale sign will have the price written in bold print but next to the price often you will see "O.B.O." (Or Best Offer) which is essentially saying to all potential buyers "do not pay me what I want for this car, instead pay me what you want to pay me." You give up all your negotiating power when you add O.B.O. Never do that ever even if you are not firm on your price, don't let them know that. All too often people will just pay you what you want, but if you have OBO or best offer on the for-sale sign, then you will never get full price. Nobody will ever say Oh, you want $10,000 for your car, I see you got best offer on the sign, but I just want to pay you full price out of the kindness of my heart. Another rule is never to buy things from a happy seller; you want to buy things from sellers who don't want to sell it, that kind of hints at the fact that they are desperate and also that it's a good item because they want to keep it. Be mindful because sellers will use this tactic to sell you junk as well. Buying things at auction such as foreclosed properties are sometimes good deals because the previous owners probably did not want to leave meaning the house may be in fair condition. There are times when the best deal is not when Johnny is still living in the property especially when he loves the house he's going to fight with you for the price whether he can afford the mortgage/taxes or not. Now there are other times when its more beneficial for the owner to still be in the property because you could probably negotiate with him to pay his back taxes, assume his mortgage, etc. thus circumventing the foreclosure process altogether.

If you want to buy a car, when you go to look at the car and test drive it, do not go smiling from ear to ear. Don't look at the interior and say, "oh I love it" or pop the hood and say "wow I never heard a motor sound this good," the Bible says "a fool uttereth everything that's on his mind." This kind of behavior suggests to the seller that he is not compelled to negotiate with you, especially now that he knows how much you like it. Always make it seem as if you have other prospects and you are just looking at cars right now. This way they must sweeten the deal in order to get your cash.

If a seller is desperate, you are going to know it because they're not really going to want you to leave especially if they know you have the cash.

Bargaining Power

It is one thing (or in some cases several things) that control negotiations, forcing the person on the other side to bend to the other persons will.

The person with the loudest voice in the room has bargaining power. The person with nothing to lose but everything to gain has the bargaining power. Look at it like this, let's say you need a kidney transplant or you're going to die soon now, the person in the room with your blood type who's contemplating selling you his or her kidney has the bargaining power, they walk up to you and ask "how much is it worth to you"?

Bargaining power can be the difference of hundreds of dollars, thousands of dollars, or millions of dollars because he that has it is saying "I have something that's worth more than what you're trying to give me" or Bargaining power is that thing that says "I have something that you need to have and nobody else can give it to you meaning you can't get it anywhere but here"! It works on both sides of the table as well but whoever has it is in the best position to make the deal.

When a rapper, singer, comedian, or any entertainer for that matter sits down with an entertainment company to sign a contract, the person that gets the best deal is the person with the most bargaining power. The YouTube sensation who created a new dance then posted a video that went viral and now has millions of views, the record company flies him or her out; sits them in an office and says, "hey we saw your video and we like it, we want to sign you to a deal, put you on billboards, in movies, commercials etc. Now though that person has more bargaining power than the singer discovered at a karaoke bar, but the record company is still going to argue the fact that they are taking a risk on a new artist with no history. But then, you take an experienced artist that has sold millions of records and now their contract is up. While their shopping another

deal when they sit in that same office, with all new record companies, they have a history of selling records and making money for investors which turns into major bargaining power because they've already proven themselves to the point where they don't really need a record company anymore, this is bargaining power at its finest.

Super Bowl ads

Once a year, the NFL does something no other company can do, they put on a show for that attracts more viewers than any other show in the world called the Super Bowl. This event is watched by millions of people presenting the advertising opportunity of a lifetime. Ad space is sold all year round on T.V. radio, billboards, magazines, buses etc. But advertising is tricky because there is no guarantee that everyone will see your Ad. After all, people drive pass billboards and never look up, people read magazines and skip pass the advertisement to read the article, they also run to the bathroom or kitchen during the sitcom. When it comes to watching the Super Bowl, people are so excited they give their undivided attention to the TV screen for that 4-hour period that the game is on.

The NFL takes advantage of this phenomenon by charging companies a multi-million-dollar fee for each 30-second commercial that airs during the Super Bowl. Why? Because that company's product or service will be viewed by more people in that 30-second window than it would have all year through all the other forms of advertising combined. Bargaining power on steroids!!

One thing that is very important and cannot be overlooked in the world of doing deals is to watch out for crooks, the crook in others and the crook in yourself. I have been scammed many times in my life, often in my attempt to get something for nothing. If you could speak with even the richest people on Earth, they would tell you countless stories of swindlers and con artist because they believe that there is a sucker born every day.

A con artist was once asked why do you con so many people, don't you feel bad about what you do? The con artist responded, "no, the only people that I've been able to con are people that take shortcuts trying to get something for nothing or those trying to get rich quick." The people that follow the straight narrow way never fall for my tricks.

I once bought a gold chain that turned out to be fake at the mall, I was coming out of a store and a random guy saw me from afar (I must have looked green) I was young in my teens and the guys said "hey, you want to buy this gold chain and he had a tag hanging off of it that read $1300. All he wanted was $80; now in my young mind, I am thinking I'm getting over but that couldn't have been further from the truth. I gave him the money, threw on my fresh gold chain and a day or two later my neck started looking greenish so I took my new jewelry to the pawnshop and the guy scraped the gold on a black rock of some sort, looked at the color of the residue and explained to me that my new chain was worth less than a bag of pennies.

I remember buying a car and the car broke down multiple times only weeks after I bought it. I was in high school with some extra funds from God knows where and one weekend there was a party I wanted to go to, you know that one party you do not want to miss? Also, at this time, of course, it was my senior year in high school, and I wanted to show off. After getting fed up with going back and forth to the repair shop, I drove into a used car dealership to see if they would take my vehicle and allow me to trade it in for another one. They agreed and I set my eyes on a black 1987 Regal which had the body of a Grand National and anybody that knows cars knows that Grand Nationals were popular race car. So, after negotiating, I agreed to give up my car as a trade-in and make up the difference in price by paying an additional $1200. I pulled off the lot in my new car on that Friday evening headed to the hotel party. The very next morning, I woke up early with hung over only to come outside to some guys standing around my car. I immediately walk over wondering why they were walking around my new car when one of the guys asked me hey did you buy this car from the dealership on State Fair, I responded full of pride with my chest poked out like yeah that's right!

He was like, awe man, we were gone buy this car. Me, being lifted with even more pride feeling geek thinking to myself "yes I got the car and y'all ain't get it"! Then the guy said, Man, how much did you pay? Being reluctant, I declined to tell him my low price but what he said next made my heart drop…. He said the guy at the dealership was going to sell them the car for $600. At that moment, my stomach started hurting and I instantly developed a headache. I sat on the curb thinking about how I gave this crook my car that I paid $1200 for with another $1200 for a Regal that he was going to sell for $600. Lesson learned was I did not know how to negotiate, but I will say that was like one of the last times I can remember being played out of my money.

CHAPTER 10

I CAN'T HEAR YOU

"Go from the presence of a foolish man, when thou perceivest not in him the lips of knowledge".

Proverbs 14:7

Surround yourself with positive people and stay away from broke people who are comfortable in their position. Find out what broke people read and do not read it. Find out where broke people hang out and make it a point not to go there.

Will Smith is quoted saying, "You are who you associate with. Look around at your five closest friends and that is who you are. If you do not want to be that person, you know what you got to do."

According to a report published by the NAACP (National Association for the Advancement of Colored People), they discovered the following: "A dollar circulates in Asian communities for a month, in Jewish communities approximately 20 days and white communities 17 days. How long does a dollar circulate in the black community? 6 hours!!! The minute that paycheck or income tax check touches the hands of African Americans, we find the nearest liquor store, shopping mall, casino or restaurant to start our next buying frenzy until we spend every penny.

African American buying power is at 1.1 Trillion, and yet only two cents of every dollar an African American spends in this country goes to black-owned businesses."

A. Things Broke people say

"Many therefore refuse to lend for other men's ill dealing, fearing to be defrauded".

Ecclesiasticus 29:7

1. Maaaannn Johnny is stingy as hell.

2. Ask Johnny; he always got some money.

3. Imma pay you back this time...I promise.

4. I ain't gone have no money till Friday, that's when I get paid.

5. I cannot wait till I get my paycheck.

6. I can't wait till I get my income tax returns.

7. He always talking bout he ain't got no money, he got it.

8. That's alright though; he bet not ever ask me for nothing else.

9. That's all you had to say.

10. I keep some money in my pockets.

11. Here, there go yo lil funky $20!

12. I know not to ask you for nothing else!

13. I think he got paid today.

14. If I hit that Mega Millions tonight, it's over!

15. I might call-off today; I do not feel like going to work. I am tired of that job.

16. It is too cold. I am calling-off.

17. It is too hot I'm calling off.

18. Its Friday don't nobody want to be cooped up in that job all day.

19. Its Monday already, uh work.

20. Next time I get some money.....

21. Yea I know its $5, but I needs all mine!!

22. Broke people will call year after year asking to borrow money, but they will never call to ask for info on how they can better their financial situation.

B. Holidays & Celebrations

Throughout the year, many people celebrate various holidays based on their religious beliefs, country or heritage. Those celebrations may or may not be costly on their own but if you add up the total bill at the end of the year for most people it will look something like this:

- *New Year's Day $250*

- *Valentine's Day $200*

- *Easter $250*

- *Mother's Day $200*

- *Memorial Day $250*

- *Father's Day $150*

- *Independence Day (4th of July) $400*

- *Labor Day $150*

- *Halloween $200*

- *Thanksgiving $225*

- *Christmas $1000*

- *New Year's Eve $250*

- *Birthday $500*

- *Family & friends' birthdays $1000+*

- *Total=$5025*

These numbers are conservative at best, so if you have kids, you may want to add. If you have a spouse, you may want to add, if you have a big family or a lot of friends you may want to add, if you're in a sorority or fraternity you may want to add and if you are just an all-around extravagant person then of course, you should add. On the other hand, if you do not celebrate holidays, you can deduct these expenses. As for me, I celebrate the High Holy days in the Bible (Passover, Hanukkah, Sabbath, etc.) and we all come together as a family so, for the most part, it's not that expensive.

CHAPTER 11

GROWTH IS A STATE OF MIND

I wise man once said [Small minds discuss "people;" Average minds discuss "events," but Great minds discuss "ideas"]

Meaning small-minded people are always talking about other people, people they know, people they don't know, people they wish they never met and so on but their mind is never on themselves which is why they can't get ahead in life.

Average minded people mostly discuss events like "remember the time when we did this or went there," a back down memory lane kind of thing. Their mind has not been reduced to talking about people all day, but it hasn't elevated to the point where those memories spark ideas.

Great minds think alike, we have all heard that saying once or twice in our life and it's true. Growth is a state of mind. You got to be focused all the time. You got to know what is going on around you, when your bills are due, how much are you spending on bills each month, what your total expenses are each year? This way, throughout the year, you can cut corners in order to save money. For instance, if you know you spend $1200 annually on a particular product each, make sure throughout the year when you buy that item you look for deals, discounts and wholesale opportunities.

You must be in the growth state of mind at all times because you have to be focused on growing and protecting your net worth with every purchase you make, every person you talk to, everywhere that you go, everything that you do has to be geared towards achieving that goal. A lot of people wake up every day with no goals. They may have 10-year or 20-year goals but nothing shorter mainly because they do not understand that goals get accomplished day by day. Little by little, something gets accomplished everyday towards reaching those goals. Remember a 15-year goal is nothing more than (3) 5-year goals completed one at a time.

Most people never take the time to know themselves, meaning if you asked them a question about themselves, they would most likely lie to you, though most will do it unknowingly. Just try it, find someone in your life that you know is lazy and ask him/her if they are lazy, they are going to tell you no. They are going to tell you no because people are programmed to tell you lies about themselves versus telling you the truth. They're programmed to tell you what you want to hear versus telling you the truth because they're afraid of what you might think about them or they think they can change your perception of them by their words and not their actions. Most people have not learned their lifestyle, so they really don't know who they are. Here is an example of what I'm talking about, the man that is unemployed and struggling prays for a job, begs for a job, he asks everyone he knows who does have a job if their job hiring? Could they put in a good word for him, he sends his resumes everywhere then he gets the interview. He is in the interview as pleasant as possible practically saying he'll do anything for work; he'll be available anytime, any day, any shift. Six months later he's on the job and the boss can't get him to work, he's missing days, he doesn't want to come in on time when he does come in, he's the employee standing in the corner saying, I'm not doing that, I am not doing anything, so nothing gets done on his watch but the bare minimum. Why, because he does not know who he is, he doesn't know what he wants. He never wanted the job in the first place. He is not a worker. What he is, is a complainer. There are many people that hate their job, but they know who they are, they know where they are going, they go to work because they know that job is a means to an end. Many of us must do what we don't want to do for a brief period so that we can do what we want to do for the rest of our lives. Whether it is starting your own business, becoming an investor buying properties to become a property owner, or things of that nature.

Some people are born with the growth state of mind, but most must develop it. When trying to help others, you must wait until their mentally ready. If somebody is not ready to grow mentally, spiritually or physically and you try to force motivation on them, they will resent you. This could cause problems in your relationship if not the ending.

Most importantly, you must get away from these types of people because they are dream killers, it is bad enough that they won't grow but if you stick around, they'll bring you down with them. Thinking outside the box is particularly important; you cannot think like everybody else. I got a friend who is from the ghettos of Detroit who sells horses while most people I know got involved with animal's sell pit bulls and rottweilers. He sells horses. His family has a farm where he builds stables for the horses. He also linked up with a few more of our friends and now they buy and sell lambs.

Another friend of mine has an eBay account where he sells used computers. Some of them work, some of them don't but either way this guy makes more money than some people with a computer science degree. He tried to get me involved saying I should start my own computer resale business, so I drove up to his shop in Pontiac to buy some laptops. When he went to the back, he came out with two stacks of the most atrocious looking laptops I have ever seen I mean they were horrible looking; some were all broken up, some didn't even have screens or keyboards. In my mind, I'm thinking what the hell is this, but I trusted him, so I paid him $100 or so and left. I'm riding home thinking man why did I just throw away $100 I could have found something else to do with that hundred, but as an investor you must think outside the box. He told me to set up an eBay account and just post all the laptops with some crazy description like "parts, not working, repair, never tested, etc. I posted the computers online and 1-week later, I probably tripled or quadruple my money. Of course, I went back without hesitation buying 50-60 laptops and this time they were in much better shape, so much so that I made enough money to pay my property taxes that year with money left over to invest.

I tell this story to show you how thinking creatively using a growth state of mind can and will bring you revenue that you never expected.

Success?

You must look within yourself to know what success is. Success cannot be identified by looking at someone else.

The biggest mistake people make is measuring their failures by someone else's success; this is true for many reasons. You may look at the accomplishments of others but if you were to ask them how they feel about their achievements, they might tell you that they are not where they set out to be.

CHAPTER 12

ROLEX TIME

"To every thing there is a season, and a time to every purpose under the heaven."

Ecclesiastes 3:1

The past is a Memory, the future is a Dream, all we have is Right now, Today!!

What does the billionaire and the bum have in common? Time....24 hours every single day. Only thing is one will use that time to make a fortune and the other will use it to make excuses. Time is the most valuable asset on the planet and it is just like money, the only difference is YOU place the value on it, but you can't touch it, only use it. If it is worthless to you, then it will show in everything you do, say, every place you go and ultimately what you become. Also, if it is valuable to you, it will show in everything you say, do, as well as places you go. Time & money are the only commodities that can be used to acquire value and they are used interchangeably.

You can buy time: Your car is set to be repossessed and your home is set to be foreclosed on but you produce enough money (not to pay them off) to buy you extra time.

You can waste time: Some people go to college and have no idea what they want to become so the change their majors twice then graduate and go into a profession that has nothing to do with what they majored in...complete waste of time. You meet someone and develop feelings for that person build a relationship for 6 months, 1 year or more only to find out they were no good after all...major waste of time.

You can be robbed of your time: For instance, you go over a friend house to visit and they ask you to take them somewhere and since they are your friend, you do it. On the way, they bombard you with conversations about nothing only to arrive at the destination and leave you in the car for 30 minutes. They finally come back and hands you $5 for gas thanking you for taking them to pick up their phone charger. You can never get that time back though they could have gotten a charger from anywhere. Be mindful of these people, they are all around you.

The more time you spend on reading, studying, watching inspirational videos, listening to audio on self-help, etc. the more value you will have in your life. On the other hand, the more time you spend hanging with friends, partying, shopping, watching TV, the more you will struggle financially and the harder it will be for you to become successful. It has been said that you should go to bed smarter than you were when you woke up....and there is no way you can do that watching cable or hanging out with negative friends all the time.

To show you time it is worth more, let's say when you turned 30 years old, I offered you

$1,000,000 dollars or (time) 100 years which one would you pick? Most people would say the $1,000,000 but very few would choose the 100 years. If we viewed both choices under a microscope, the 100 years would prove to have enormously more value.

$1,000,000 - For starters, this amount is worthless without "time" because you would not be able to spend it nor invest it. You have no idea when you are going to die, so you live like there is no tomorrow. You did not accumulate it from hard work so you will not appreciate it nor have a chance to get the skills to keep it, so you lack the financial resources to protect or grow it. Everyone you know will ask to borrow money; you will give it to them, they will never pay you back, so you will go broke helping people. On the other side, you will tell them no they will get mad and you will lose all your friends and family. You will try to buy things above your means because after all this money is a lump sum, not steady income so you will never be able to pay the upkeep, taxes or maintenance on the luxury things you buy.

Time (100 years) - You have all the time in the world to develop the tools to help you become financially secure. You have the time to build yourself spiritually and get closer to God, find out his plan for you and carry out those goals which at the end of the day are far more important.

CHAPTER 13

DEBT/CREDIT/OPM

"The rich ruleth over the poor, and the borrower is servant to the lender".

Proverbs 22:7

"Lend to thy neighbour in time of his need, and pay thou thy neighbour again in due season".

Ecclesiasticus 29:2

The words on the American dollar says "For all debts public and private" but unfortunately, money is dead since it is not backed by anything. It is a medium of exchange that allows you to buy things, but it is not backed by anything meaning the only value it has is the value the Federal Reserve puts on it through supply and interest rates. If it is an abundance of supply people will spend, spend, spend. On the other hand, if there is a shortage of money in circulation, then people will hoard their cash. Either way, it is all debt.... cash, coins, credit, etc. it is debt passed from one to another. Private banks pass debt to central banks, central banks pass debt to commercial banks, commercial banks pass debt to the people and in turn, the people pass debt to each other. Here is how it really works:

You come to do work on my house and afterwards, you asked me to pay you something of value, so I say "I don't have anything here but take this money as an I.O.U. Now what will happen is you're going to take that bill I gave you (that promissory note) and go to the store to purchase an item, the store clerk tells you how much it cost then you tell him you don't have it but you explain how somebody whom you worked for owes you money and gave you a promissory note. You then give the store clerk the note thus binding you to "pay to the bearer upon demand." Nobody ever gets the actual principle; only that we just keep passing that debt on and on. Speaking of the dollar, there has been so many printed that it just depreciates in value. So, by the time the last person in the cycle goes to redeem the true value of that note promised in the beginning, it is much less than what the original person should have received. The sad truth is someone will end up buying a home with those notes they accumulated over the years only to fall on hard times and ultimately lose that home to the government, making the government the only winner in this vicious economic cycle to retain an actual asset of value off the blood, sweat and tears of the people through the printing of money backed by nothing.

Debit, credit, loans, etc. are all forms of O.P.M. (Other People's Money). Anytime you use capital to purchase something that's not yours it's OPM, whether it comes from Visa, MasterCard, Capital One, American Express, Bank of America, local credit union, mother, Father, the guy next door, business partner, co-worker wherever it comes from it's all OPM. If it did not come out of your bank account or from under your mattress, it is not your money its OPM. The only difference is the terms. Banks have certain terms, credit card company's got different terms, friends and family may have more lenient terms, private investors, hard money lenders individually will carry different terms.

Interest rates may vary, time limits may vary, there could be all kinds of variations depending on who you go through, where you get the loan from when you signed for the money and why you are asking.

Let's say you needed a loan to purchase an $80,000, car you will be seeking auto financing with a 3-5 year window to pay it off but then if you turn right around and go back into the same bank to tell them you needed to borrow that same $80,000 to purchase a home, they will require you to sign a 30-year fixed mortgage contract. Why? Who knows, maybe they want to milk your bank account for 30 years' worth of interest payments or maybe they know you will only pay for 5-10 years then stop, that way they can foreclose on that property for non-payment and redo the process all over again with someone else. This is how banks sneak their way into the real estate business by turning you into an agent, they let you drive all over the city, find the house, pay for an appraisal, fix it up then give you a loan they know you can't afford and take the house away once you default.

Your friends and family may lend you money and you might not pay them back but you get to tell him stuff like "hey I ain't forgot about you, I ain't got it and this may go on for two or three years. You won't try that with a bank because you know the bank is smarter than your family and they made you sign a contract that says that you give up ownership or give up title to whatever asset that you purchase whether car, house, boat, etc. and they can come to repossess that house, car or boat. Your friends on the other hand cannot do that, all they can do is be upset and be mad, they might not deal with you anymore, or tell you they are not loaning you any more money.

This whole country was built on OPM. All the major industries and companies, whether private or public were built on OPM. When a company goes public, that means it went from a private company to a public company by way of offering shares to the public that the public can purchase on the open market. That company then uses that money to grow and run the business. Before they went public, they went through different rounds of funding raising capital. It starts with someone looking at an idea somebody else came up with in their basement. Afterwards, they go through the first round of raising money (capital) and this is where they asked Grandma, mom, dad, their brothers, friends, co-workers, etc. to hopefully acquire the seed money to maybe obtain copyrights, business plans, or rough drafts. Once that money has been spent they move into the second round of fundraising either through crowdfunding, GoFundMe, Kickstarter, etc., This round is usually funded by what are called angel investors but the second round is where you run into venture capitalists, these are people who actually sit around and look to invest in ideas, startups, small businesses etc. At this stage, most businesses are yet to really take off as it may be that their just past the inception stage, maybe they have a working prototype and just need to get manufactured or probably just started to get it manufactured. It could be that they need some marketing and distribution or a back-office that will help with streamlining international logistics overseas.

Venture capitalists can help with everything from securing patents to opening a chain of brick and mortar franchises. They can be instrumental in helping you hire a team of employees, provide lawyers for drafting, protection or litigation. It is all kind of different reasons why people go through these different rounds but remember it's all OPM. OPM is the fuel that runs this capitalistic society which is why hard money and private money is so available when it comes to real estate and you can get in the matter of days sometimes hours. These individuals give out short term loans to real estate investors to buy and build properties and it works for them because their money is doing exactly what they need it to do, grow. Real estate investors love them because they can go and get somebody else's money and make a profit off it, return it with a little interest and now they have an asset that will bring them an infinite return.

Say for instance, I go to a hard money lender and I ask for $50,000, then I take that $50,000 that they gave me, and I buy a house that is worth $180,000 after repairs. I go to that same hard/private money lender and ask for $40,000 more to fix it up. After the repairs are complete I put the house on the market for $180,000 ($165,000 if I want it to go quick), it sells, then I pay back the $90,000 I borrowed + plus interest and pocket the remaining $75,000-$80,000 whatever is left minus expenses. I would then put that money in other properties, stocks, crypto or whatever because the rule is to compound the profit and under no circumstances ever go under money.

Just for the record, no!! I am not rich nor am I broke, what I am is a man who has traveled all over these United States and a few countries outside of here many times and rarely for vacation. I've known millionaires, celebrities and many entrepreneurs and I have been privileged to soak up more game (wisdom) than I can put in this book. I've narrowed the bulk of information down to 13 chapters that will definitely change your life no matter what tax bracket your in.

Purchase **FAMOUS BOARD GAME** only $19.99

www.famousboardgame.com

We also offer:

FINANCIAL COACHING SERVICES

CREDIT REPAIR SERVICES

OTHER BUSINESS SERVICES

to inquire contact us @

248-277-5590 office

313-778-8141 cell

jeriah@neverundermoney.com

Made in the USA
Monee, IL
06 August 2020

37729404R00101